Terrorism

David M. Haugen and Matthew J. Box, Book Editors

Bruce Glassman, Vice President
Bonnie Szumski, Publisher
Helen Cothran, Managing Editor
Scott Barbour, Series Editor

GREENHAVEN PRESS
An imprint of Thomson Gale, a part of The Thomson Corporation

THOMSON
＊ ™
GALE

Detroit • New York • San Francisco • San Diego • New Haven, Conn.
Waterville, Maine • London • Munich

For more information, contact
Greenhaven Press
27500 Drake Rd.
Farmington Hills, MI 48331-3535
Or you can visit our Internet site at http://www.gale.com

Cover credit: © Yossi Zamir/FLASH 90/Reuters/CORBIS. Victims of a suicide bombing aboard a bus in Jerusalem receive first aid.

LIBRARY OF CONGRESS CATALOGING-IN-PUBLICATION DATA

Terrorism / David M. Haugen and Matthew J. Box, book editors.
   p. cm. — (Social issues firsthand)
Includes bibliographical references and index.
ISBN 0-7377-2501-X (lib. : alk. paper)
   1. Terrorism. 2. Terrorists—Psychology. 3. Victims of terrorism—Psychology.
I. Haugen, David M., 1969– . II. Box, Matthew J. III. Series.
HV6431.T4569 2006
303.6'25—dc22
                                            2005040218

Printed in the United States of America

CONTENTS

CHAPTER 1: WHAT MOTIVATES A TERRORIST?

CHAPTER 2: WITNESSES AND SURVIVORS OF TERRORIST ACTIONS

Social issues are often viewed in abstract terms. Pressing challenges such as poverty, homelessness, and addiction are viewed as problems to be defined and solved. Politicians, social scientists, and other experts engage in debates about the extent of the problems, their causes, and how best to remedy them. Often overlooked in these discussions is the human dimension of the issue. Behind every policy debate over poverty, homelessness, and substance abuse, for example, are real people struggling to make ends meet, to survive life on the streets, and to overcome addiction to drugs and alcohol. Their stories are ubiquitous and compelling. They are the stories of everyday people—perhaps your own family members or friends—and yet they rarely influence the debates taking place in state capitols, the national Congress, or the courts.

The disparity between the public debate and private experience of social issues is well illustrated by looking at the topic of poverty. Each year the U.S. Census Bureau establishes a poverty threshold. A household with an income below the threshold is defined as poor, while a household with an income above the threshold is considered able to live on a basic subsistence level. For example, in 2003 a family of two was considered poor if its income was less than $12,015; a family of four was defined as poor if its income was less than $18,810. Based on this system, the bureau estimates that 35.9 million Americans (12.5 percent of the population) lived below the poverty line in 2003, including 12.9 million children below the age of eighteen.

Commentators disagree about what these statistics mean. Social activists insist that the huge number of officially poor Americans translates into human suffering. Even many families that have incomes above the threshold, they maintain, are likely to be struggling to get by. Other commentators insist that the statistics exaggerate the problem of poverty in the United States. Compared to people in developing countries, they point out, most so-called poor families have a high quality of life. As stated by journalist Fidelis Iyebote, "Cars are owned by 70 percent of 'poor' households. . . . Color televisions belong to 97 percent of the 'poor' [and] videocassette recorders belong to nearly 75 percent. . . . Sixty-four percent have microwave ovens, half own a stereo system, and over a quarter possess an automatic dishwasher."

However, this debate over the poverty threshold and what it means is likely irrelevant to a person living in poverty. Simply put, poor people do not need the government to tell them whether they are poor. They can see it in the stack of bills they cannot pay. They are aware of it when they are forced to choose between paying rent or buying food for their children. They become painfully conscious of it when they lose their homes and are forced to live in their cars or on the streets. Indeed, the written stories of poor people define the meaning of poverty more vividly than a government bureaucracy could ever hope to. Narratives composed by the poor describe losing jobs due to injury or mental illness, depict horrific tales of childhood abuse and spousal violence, recount the loss of friends and family members. They evoke the slipping away of social supports and government assistance, the descent into substance abuse and addiction, the harsh realities of life on the streets. These are the perspectives on poverty that are too often omitted from discussions over the extent of the problem and how to solve it.

Greenhaven Press's Social Issues Firsthand series provides a forum for the often-overlooked human perspectives on society's most divisive topics of debate. Each volume focuses on one social issue and presents a collection of ten to sixteen narratives by those who have had personal involvement with the topic. Extra care has been taken to include a diverse range of perspectives. For example, in the volume on adoption, readers will find the stories of birth parents who have given up their children for adoption, adoptive parents, and adoptees themselves. After exposure to these varied points of view, the reader will have a clearer understanding that adoption is an intense, emotional experience full of joyous highs and painful lows for all concerned.

Each book in the series contains several features that enhance its usefulness, including an in-depth introduction, an annotated table of contents, bibliographies for further research, a list of organizations to contact, and a thorough index. These elements—combined with the poignant voices of people touched by tragedy and triumph—make the Social Issues Firsthand series a valuable resource for research on today's topics of political discussion.

Writing to Cope with Terrorism

On the morning of September 11, 2001, when Arab terrorists hijacked two commercial airliners and crashed them into the twin towers of New York's World Trade Center, the resulting catastrophe was earth-shattering. Including those on board the airplanes and those who perished when the towers subsequently collapsed, nearly three thousand people lost their lives in the attack. Though not the first, it was the deadliest single incident of terrorism the world had yet seen. By any standard, the tragedy was difficult to comprehend. Even in times of war, rarely do so many individuals die in one place at one time. Those who were left alive—whether survivors of the attack or even people who watched the horror unfold on television screens halfway around the world—had no recourse but to absorb the momentousness and chilling reality of the event. They also had to come to grips with the fact that, on that same day, the same group of terrorists had steered another airplane into the Pentagon in Washington, D.C., and forced the crash of a fourth plane in Pennsylvania. These attacks added more than 220 lives to the already staggering death toll on that September morning.

Commenting one year after the World Trade Center tragedy, Les Aaron, a political commentator, stated,

> How can anyone who witnessed such a thing be not unchanged by the experience? Thoughts of that chilling day will never go away; they bring to mind the essential evanescence of things, the fragility of life. In their randomness and suddenness, we are forced to come to grips with the reality that there are no guarantees. What was there this morning will not necessarily be there upon our return. No matter how hard we pray.[1]

Aaron's words reflect much of America's reaction to the events of September 11, but they could also be applied to the experiences of survivors and witnesses of any terrorist attack. Just reviewing the last decade, Aaron could have been speaking of the 168 people who were killed when a bomb exploded outside the Murrah Federal Building in Oklahoma City in April 1995, or of the thousands of unsuspecting victims of the March 1995 sarin gas attacks on board Tokyo's crowded commuter trains, or even of the scores of bystanders killed in the myriad suicide bombings or car bomb explosions that happen each year in Israel. Every tragedy of this kind destroys lives outright and scars the survivors and other witnesses who struggle to make sense of the brutality of terrorist acts.

WRITING AS EMOTIONAL RELEASE

One way survivors and others try to make sense out of the carnage and death is to write or speak about them. Typically in the wake of almost any terrorist event comes a host of personal, eyewitness accounts delivered by individuals who cheated fate and escaped death or by those who felt compelled to define the meaning of the terrible event as they understood it. Professor Louise DeSalvo, one of the proponents of writing as a method of healing, strongly believes that recording one's thoughts and sharing them is a useful tool for defining the personal meaning of tragic events, as well as helping one through the grieving process associated with them. In her book *Writing as a Way of Healing*, DeSalvo cites a 1986 study by psychology professor James W. Pennebaker and Sandra Beall that concluded (in DeSalvo's words) "that simply . . . venting one's feelings about trauma or only describing traumas isn't sufficient to improve health. *To improve health, we must write detailed accounts, linking feelings with events.* The more writing succeeds as narrative—by being detailed, organized, compelling, vivid, lucid—the more health and emotional benefits are derived from writing."[2]

DeSalvo, Pennebaker, Beall, and other writers and psychologists have noted that writing is a method of purging the mind and body of pent-up emotions. Survivors of and witnesses to terrorist attacks have the need to dispel their anger, frustration, grief, and despair, and therefore many choose to write out their feelings as a form of therapy. Henriette Anne Klauser, a writer and educator who attended a therapeutic writing workshop four days after the World Trade Center attack, recalls the benefits of the session in her book *With Pen in Hand: The Healing Power of Writing:* "We took our sadness and our rage and put it on the page where it could not harm us or anybody else. As we expressed our deepest feelings without reserve in poetry and prose, we felt the power of our words begin to draw out some of the pain from our hearts and replace it with hope."[3]

NO LONGER A VICTIM

Others use their writing as a way of bringing order and sense to the fragmentary way in which most people experience something both terrible and unfamiliar. As one New Yorker said of his outlook in the wake of the attack on the World Trade Center, "It began with a feeling of surreal madness . . . like I'm living in a war zone; this turned to an uncomfortable silence—walking by others on the street knowing that it's on the top of everyone's mind but no one knows what to do or say."[4] As DeSalvo, Klauser, and others have attested, framing that "feeling of surreal madness" with a narrative gives structure to the horrific act and its consequences and reduces the trauma to a more manageable state. It also allows for the witness to reestablish a dialogue with the countless others who seemingly do not know what to say about the event or their feelings about it.

Not knowing what to say about a tragic event often leaves many victims and bystanders feeling powerless. Placing the details of an event into an ordered, recognizable narrative returns power to the writer. Tim, a Seattle native whom Klauser discusses in her book, lost friends in the World Trade Center disaster. He was so shocked by the news and by the event itself that he could not function for days after the tragedy. Eventually, though, Tim brought out his writer's notebook and collected his thoughts. In questioning himself about why he would choose to write at all about the pain and loss, Tim wrote, "I can build, manipulate, structure, order and create the ideas that fill my notebooks. My world is in these pages; I am the master of it, and I can control it. I can't control my feelings, but I can create order within the blue lines of my Mead notebook."[5] Writing for Tim, as for other witnesses to tragic events, brought an empowering sensation that he was no longer a passive victim of terrorism; even if it was only by writing a few lines or pages in a diary, he would no longer retreat from the world.

SPEAKING OUT AGAINST TERRORISM

Sometimes those affected by a terrorist act want not only to escape victimization but to become active in the political and social remedies to terrorism. These crusaders use their personal narratives as political weapons against the very fear and anger caused by terrorist attacks. Eliad Moreh, a victim of the bombing of Jerusalem's Hebrew University in July 2002 that killed nine people and injured eighty-six others, decided that she could not remain silent after having witnessed such an atrocious act, one that scarred her physically and emotionally and took the life of one of her friends. She embarked on a tour of U.S. college campuses to detail her own experiences and speak out against terrorism. Moreh told the *Northeastern News*, the newspaper of Boston's Northeastern University, where she spoke in 2003, "I . . . felt after I survived [the bombing] that I received life as a present. . . . I felt dedicated towards life and the life of my [deceased] friend. This is my way to fight terror; this is my way to say I will not be a passive victim."[6]

While some like Moreh go on speaking tours against terrorism, other writers or speakers (often those who did not suffer loss in an attack) direct their righteousness into increased patriotism when it seems obvious that a terrorist act was targeting a whole nation and its ideology. After the September 11 attacks, the 2004 train bombings in Madrid (which the Spanish government was quick to blame on Basque separatists), and even suicide bombings in the Middle East, many newspaper editorials and personal-narrative e-mails to news Web sites ended with sentiments that these terrorist attacks failed in their attempts to humble entire nations and instead fostered a greater sense of unity and commitment to bring the perpetrators to justice.

AN IMPORTANT HISTORICAL RECORD

Many of the personal narratives collected in this anthology display variations of the aforementioned writing strategies. Some of the terror victims seek to give order to chaotic events; others relate personal grief and loss. Regardless of the motivations, these survivor and eyewitness testimonies expose the bravery and compassion of those who faced nightmarish catastrophes. There are tales of rescue and selfless efforts to save other victims, and there are stories that show the powerlessness of not being able to help those in need. None of these narrators applaud their own heroism; in fact, the majority of survivors express a wish that such tragedies not be repeated.

In contrast, this anthology also includes the words of some of those accused of perpetrating acts of terrorism. These testimonies reveal motivations of a different character. They often insist that their victimization by despotic governments—that is, powerful forces beyond their control—pushed them into committing heinous acts of revenge. While these perpetrators may not gloat over their acts, they often express no remorse for their victims. Their written testimonials attempt to justify their acts but may also be a means to assuage their own feelings of guilt by displacing the blame for their acts on some inchoate, unconquerable authority.

Whether victim, bystander, or perpetrator, the narrators of the tales in this anthology have left important historical records of these terrorist events. Instead of providing death tolls and dates, these personal accounts expose the human side of tragedy. They narrow the distance between writer and reader, allowing the latter to vicariously experience the range of emotions without being put in harm's way. As DeSalvo writes, "Writing about difficulties enables us to discover the wholeness of things, the connectedness of human experience. We understand that our greatest shocks do not separate us from humankind. Instead, through expressing ourselves, we establish our connection with others and with the world."[7] Perhaps, then, the written word may be—as Moreh suggests—the ultimate weapon against terrorism.

NOTES

1. Les Aaron, "Bearing Witness to 9/11," October 28, 2002. www.mike hersh.com/Bearing_Witness_to_911.shtml.

2. Louise DeSalvo, *Writing as a Way of Healing: How Telling Our Stories Transforms Our Lives*. Boston: Beacon, 1999, p. 22.

3. Henriette Anne Klauser, *With Pen in Hand: The Healing Power of Writing*. Cambridge, MA: Perseus, 2003, p. x.

4. Quoted in BBC News, "The Survivors' Stories," October 4, 2001. http://news.bbc.co.uk/1/hi/talking_point/1544197.stm.

5. Quoted in Klauser, *With Pen in Hand*, p. 110.

6. Quoted in Bradley Rosenberg, "Hebrew U Bomb Blast Survivor Tells Her Story," *Northeastern News*, February 26, 2003. www.nu-news.com/news/2003/02/26/News/Hebrew.U.Bomb.Blast.Survivor.Tells.Her.Story-386187.shtml.

7. DeSalvo, *Writing as a Way of Healing*, p. 43.

CHAPTER 1

What Motivates a Terrorist?

Fighting the Oppressor Is Doing the Work of God

by Hizbullah

Hizbullah—or the Party of God—is a Lebanese spiritual and political organization of Shiite Muslims that gained world recognition when one of its branches took responsibility for the bombings of a U.S. Marine barracks in Beirut in 1983. Subsequently, the group hijacked TWA flight 847 over Greece in June 1985 and carried out attacks on Jewish centers in Argentina in the early 1990s. The organization perpetrated these and other terrorist acts in protest of the U.S.-sanctioned, Israeli occupation of the Lebanese homeland. Hizbullah seeks to prove to Israel and the United States that the people of Lebanon will not allow their nation to be occupied without a fight.

In 1997, upon a visit to Lebanon, Pope John Paul II received a message from Hizbullah stating its justification for taking up arms against Israeli oppression and Israel's American backers. The following article, an excerpt from this message, provides an explanation of Hizbullah's motives. It is the organization's contention that armed resistance to occupation is a "divine and human right." The letter, therefore, attempts to invoke the pontiff's grace toward Hizbullah's cause by investing it with spiritual significance. Made plain by the author's rhetoric, it is the hope of Hizbullah to gain a powerful and pious ally in its struggle.

I n the Name of Allah Most Gracious Most Merciful
The honorable Supreme Pontiff Pope John Paul the Second:
Greetings,
As you perform your pastoral visit to Lebanon, allow us to address you with these words on issues and affairs that certainly fall within the framework of your concerns and are essential to the existence and future of our people.

Hizbullah, letter to Pope John Paul II, http://almashriq.hiof.no, May 1997.

FAITH, A NECESSITY FOR HUMANITY

Honorable Supreme Pontiff,

Your Eminence, with what you represent, presides over one of the religious authorities in the world that is concerned about developing the human being's direction towards the Supreme Lord, the Creator and the One who causes death, the One who originates the creation and the One who reproduces it, and about establishing the relation between human beings on the grounds of Divine values that translate spiritual sublimity into social ethics that would enable the human society to live under a degree of justice, security and peace.

You know, no doubt, that might and victory have become the criteria of relationships between individuals and groups.

The international political developments came not to enhance the human being's belief in his or her Lord as natural harmony with the human innate character and the basis for salvation, but to increase the power of the prevalent materialistic trends and their feeling of strength.

The atmosphere of globalization and the spread of the values of market economy and competitiveness disassemble the last concrete restraints that have been required by the social circumstances of the intellectual-political conflict that had been going on during the cold war in such a manner that social relationships within the scope of countries themselves and at the international relations' level, have become unchained by the rules that would protect the minima of the rights of the oppressed in a free dignified living; these relations started to adopt more brutal forms.

Under the increasing growth of the domination of the capital sector on economic transactions and the media, that have become a major player in influencing the cultural identity of every nation and in formulating its awareness and knowledge, the human societies are losing the restraints of balance and stability between the individuals of these societies and between one society and the other.

As no materialistic doctrine could persist as a socio-political system, the greater crises, hunger, poverty, pollution, corruption and wars, confirm the downfall of the materialistic doctrine generally and its failure in organizing the human living so as to realize its safety and development.

Today, as has always been the case we need the spirit of prophethood and mission to restore the spiritual beam of divine values in a world suffering from the crises of hunger, crime, anxiety and frustration.

An urgent mission falls upon the believers in the world: to rescue humanity from the savagery of the merciless competitiveness values and to restore humanity to the sanctuary of human values by a right word in the face of the tyrants of injustice and despotism that would be a light of hope for the wronged and oppressed who are sinking under suppression.

Depriving a human being of the right and the hope to recover it makes the dignified death more desirable to him than living in humiliation.

Defending faith values and establishing divine values in the human societies are more appropriate than the race between the people of different faiths to attract congregations and followers from their opposite lines; the believers' cooperation in solidarity is the requested position today.

LIBERATING AL-QUODS

Honorable Supreme Pontiff,

You are coming today to a region in which the tragedy has been staying for a long time; the tragedy of peoples whose free will of self-determination has been plundered; that made them fall as captives of the dominance of super powers which give precedence to their interests over the aspirations and hopes of these peoples. The tragedy reached its apex when a whole nation has been disposed from their land under the pretext of establishing a safe homeland for another people, regardless of the facts of history and geography.

The aftereffects of that tragedy are still there, and are being established as a fact intended to have the international law's legitimacy through imposing concession on the helpless to make them give up their right in all of the land in exchange for scattered patches of small parts of this ravished land, and for a lean entity.

This international approach in dealing with the Palestinian issue began to threaten al-Quods itself. This city viewed with sanctity by Moslems, being their first *kiblah* (direction to which Moslems turn in prayer) and the site to which prophet Mohammed had traveled at midnight and from there he ascended to the seven heavens in a trip that has been a symbol of the accomplishment of the faith journey and a gate to the supreme world. The city is viewed with reverence and sanctity by Christians as well. There are those, however, who want it to become an eternal capital for an aggressive racist entity that has had a history full of persecuting the followers of other faiths.

This city that is holy in the Christian conscience, and that has always stimulated the zeal of the Christian peoples, is being emptied quietly and persistently—as you know—of the Arab presence, be it Moslem or Christian, that presence is tremendously diminishing due to the systematic policy adopted against it as individuals and institutions.

Silence leads to and contributes in tightening the Israeli dominance over al-Quods and drives towards a state of nonchalance by many people in the world. Therefore, it is useful to indicate that ending the silence and terminating the nonchalance would be through initiating a clear ecclesiastic stand that calls for liberating al-Quods from the grip of the occupying Zionists and lifting the Israeli dominance off it.

FIGHTING THE OCCUPIERS IS A DIVINE AND HUMAN RIGHT

Honorable Supreme Pontiff,

This country, honored by your generous visit today, is still bereaved of a part of its soil that has been under Israeli occupation for almost two decades, besides, the scars of the seasonal massacres and daily killings are still evident in parts of the country. The groans of pain and grief have not been silenced yet.

The occupying enemy relies on tyrannical might and unlimited support from the USA that provides it with military aid and political cover.

Driven by our faith and belonging to our homeland, we found ourselves in the position of a people who has to fight the aggressor that occupies its land, as such does every free people.

We know that, in your letter on Bosnia during the civil war, you have asserted the sanctity of the right of self-defense and the legitimacy of taking up arms for that sake.

The Israeli enemy and its American ally want to make resorting to fight the occupying aggressor an illegitimate act; they have been employing their political and media resources and utilizing their capability of controlling the international public opinion institutions to make that notion prevail.

We address you, hoping that you will give the needed support to the resistance of our oppressed people that has the right to liberate its land from an unjust and tyrant enemy. The oppressed victims of the Qana, Mansouri, Sohmor, Nabatieh and other massacres and the resistance fighters who are sacrificing themselves in Southern Lebanon and West Bekaa are not less sacrificing nor is their cause less just than that of the Polish workmen in Gdansk [who opposed Communist rule in the 1980s]; for difference in faith is no reason to abate a human right. . . .

Honorable Supreme Pontiff,

As we welcome you in our beloved country Lebanon, we hope your visit will be successful and prosperous.

Hizbullah

The Hypocritical Americans Deserve Their Punishment

by Osama bin Laden

Osama bin Laden is a former Saudi Arabian businessman who now heads the terrorist organization known as al Qaeda. He is credited with being the mastermind behind several attacks on U.S. targets overseas, as well as the now-infamous September 11, 2001, attack on the World Trade Center in New York. Bin Laden's al Qaeda (meaning "the base") is dedicated to ridding Arab lands of America's presence and influence and ending Israel's occupation of Palestinian lands. Their hostile actions are founded on a belief that America's Middle East policies are an affront to Islam.

The following selection is a transcript of a video of bin Laden that was sent to al-Jazeera television, the Arab world's major news network. Al-Jazeera broadcast the tape immediately after the United States began bombing Afghanistan on October 7, 2001, in the wake of the September 11 attacks. In the video, bin Laden and other al Qaeda leaders speak of America's campaign in Iraq (since the 1991 Gulf War) as being one of many examples of Western tyranny. Furthermore, though he does not take credit for the World Trade Center attacks, bin Laden maintains that the United States cannot bemoan the fate of the victims of September 11 without first acknowledging the terror that the American government has wreaked in the Middle East. America's suffering, according to bin Laden, is a just punishment from God.

I bear witness that there is no God but Allah and that Muhammad is his messenger.

There is America, hit by God in one of its softest spots. Its greatest buildings were destroyed, thank God for that. There is America,

Osama bin Laden, "Hypocrisy Rears Its Ugly Head," *The Washington Post*, October 8, 2001.

full of fear from its north to its south, from its west to its east. Thank God for that.

WHAT AMERICA DESERVES

What America is tasting now is something insignificant compared to what we have tasted for scores of years. Our nation [the Islamic world] has been tasting this humiliation and this degradation for more than 80 years. Its sons are killed, its blood is shed, its sanctuaries are attacked, and no one hears and no one heeds.

When God blessed one of the groups of Islam, vanguards of Islam, they destroyed America. I pray to God to elevate their status and bless them.

Millions of innocent children are being killed as I speak. They are being killed in Iraq without committing any sins, and we don't hear condemnation or a *fatwa* [religious decree] from the rulers. In these days, Israeli tanks infest Palestine—in Jenin, Ramallah, Rafah, Beit Jala and other places in the land of Islam—and we don't hear anyone raising his voice or moving a limb.

When the sword comes down [on America], after 80 years, hypocrisy rears its ugly head. They deplore and they lament for those killers, who have abused the blood, honor and sanctuaries of Muslims. The least that can be said about those people is that they are debauched. They have followed injustice. They supported the butcher over the victim, the oppressor over the innocent child. May God show them his wrath and give them what they deserve.

A CLEAR SITUATION

I say that the situation is clear and obvious. After this event, after the senior officials have spoken in America, starting with the head of infidels worldwide, President George W. Bush, and those with him. They have come out in force with their men and have turned even the countries that belong to Islam to this treachery, and they want to wag their tail at God, to fight Islam, to suppress people in the name of terrorism.

When people at the ends of the earth, Japan, were killed by their hundreds of thousands, young and old, it was not considered a war crime, it is something that has justification. Millions of children in Iraq is something that has justification. But when they lose dozens of people in Nairobi and Dar es Salaam [capitals of Kenya and Tanzania, where U.S. embassies were bombed in 1998], Iraq was struck and Afghanistan was struck. Hypocrisy stood in force behind the head of infidels worldwide, behind the cowards of this age, America and those who are with it.

These events have divided the whole world into two sides—the side of believers and the side of infidels. May God keep you away from them. Every Muslim has to rush to make his religion victorious. The winds of faith have come. The winds of change have come to eradicate oppression from the island of Muhammad, peace be upon him.

To America, I say only a few words to it and its people. I swear by God, who has elevated the skies without pillars, neither America nor the people who live in it will dream of security before we live it in Palestine, and not before all the infidel armies leave the land of Muhammad, peace be upon him.

God is great, may pride be with Islam. May peace and God's mercy be upon you.

The U.S. Government Is Tyrannical and Hypocritical

Part I: Timothy McVeigh, interviewed by Patrick Cole;
Part II: Timothy McVeigh

Timothy McVeigh was the immediate suspect in the 1995 bombing of the Alfred P. Murrah Federal Building in Oklahoma. Near the building's wreckage, FBI investigators had found an axle of the truck in which the explosives were detonated, and they successfully traced the vehicle to a Ryder rental facility that had recently released the truck to McVeigh. The subsequent hunt for the suspect did not last long. Only two days after the bombing, twenty-seven-year-old McVeigh had ironically been pulled over and arrested for a traffic violation and a weapons charge by police in the small town of Perry, just eighty miles from Oklahoma City. When the FBI arrived in Perry, McVeigh was quickly remanded to federal custody and charged with the murder of the 168 people who died in the Murrah building. Federal authorities held McVeigh in prison for a year, and then, because of the understandably biased public attitudes in Oklahoma, he was granted a change of venue and moved to Colorado to stand trial for the bombing.

On March 30, 1996, the day before he was moved to Colorado, McVeigh gave an interview to *Time* magazine reporter Patrick Cole. During their talk, excerpted in Part I of the following selection, McVeigh maintains his innocence, but he makes striking comments about his belief that the government of the United States is no longer under the control of the people. He insists that the government's conduct of war against foreign nations and its continual abridging of civil rights at home exemplifies that the rulers are far exceeding their just powers.

Even after he was found guilty on June 2, 1997, and conceded his part in the bombing, McVeigh carried on his lambasting of the government. In Part II of the following selection,

McVeigh argues that it may have been unfortunate that so many civilians (including nineteen children) died in the Oklahoma bombing, but the U.S. government is guilty of far more heinous crimes. In this tirade, published in *Media Bypass*, an alternative journal that gives voice to the militia movement and other anti-government organizations, McVeigh recounts the many instances in which the government has killed civilians in foreign countries and never been vilified as McVeigh has been. Drawing on his own experiences as a soldier in the 1991 Gulf War, McVeigh says that the U.S. government was hypocritical in condemning Iraqi leader Saddam Hussein as a killer when America is responsible for so much devastation and death both at home and abroad. Although McVeigh never stated that his beliefs on these matters motivated him to bomb the Murrah Federal Building, most analysts agree that his choice of targets revealed his deep-seated anger against a government that he thought was both tyrannical and hypocritical.

I

Time: How do you feel about our system of government?

McVeigh: I think the Constitution is the greatest document ever created by man. There are always going to be faults in an experiment, which is what it was. I believe there are faults, some of them serious, right now.

Time: Such as?

McVeigh: I think it all has to do with life, liberty and the pursuit of happiness, and the misconception that the government is obliged to provide those things or has the jurisdiction to deny them. We've gotten away from the principle that they were only created to secure those rights. And that's where, I believe, much of the trouble has surfaced.

Time: You were friends with James Nichols and he told us that you both discussed government and freedom and you have similar views? What is your feeling about our system of tax?

McVeigh: I think one of the intents of the Founding Fathers in keeping to indirect taxation, and really not providing for direct taxation except in unusual circumstances, was to keep government limited. They realized that the more income the government had, the larger it would grow. Our President told us during the subcommittee hearings on crime and terrorism that we should not be focused on Ruby Ridge and Waco,[1] we should be focusing on bombs. Well, that's the tendency toward a narrow view that is contributing to the problem. Each one of these events that I've named are just symptoms. A good physician is going to examine the symptoms to find the disease. And no one's paying attention to what the disease is. They are not trying to identify it. All they're trying to do is to treat the symptoms. People have to really analyze, step back and try to think what is the cause of all this? It's all inter-related, whether it be the events I named or the growing resentment of taxation in America, obtrusive government. There is [a] larger problem.

Time: Do you think our democratic system permits a full airing out of grievances that anyone might have against the government?

McVeigh: I believe there are many checks and balances built into our system of government. However, I think many of them have been circumvented and right now you have an arrogance of attitude, an omnipotent attitude. An example would be property seizure, asset seizure. If it's unjustified, what do you have to do to get the stuff back? You have to sue. They know that people don't have the money to sue the federal government, to go up against their unlimited resources. I think another aspect to that has to do with to secure these rights, governments are instituted among men, deriving their just powers from the consent of the governed. Their just powers. I believe we've lost track of what the just power of the federal government is and what it is not. There are too many things that are being given to a democracy that shouldn't be the subject of a vote, that are inalienable rights that are not to be decided by a central government.

MILITARY

Time: Why did you join the military?

McVeigh: I wanted to see more of the world. I thought I had led a sheltered life and I pretty much had. I had never really gotten out of my hometown. I fell for the sales slogans, "Be all you can be" and "We do more before nine o'clock than most people do in a day." I said, "Alright, let's try it."

Time: What was your feelings about engaging in war? I take it when you joined the country was at peace?

McVeigh: At that time, there was no real threat except for the

---

1. Ruby Ridge, Idaho, and Waco, Texas, were the sites of violent confrontations between federal agents and armed citizens during the 1990s.

cold war. I recognized the risk, but other than that I really didn't think about it.

Time: You said you became disillusioned with war during the Gulf War experience. Could you tell me why?

McVeigh: When you're on the ground, and you're not in the rear of the action, you're right up front, you realize that the people fighting are no different from you. They've got a wife and kids at home, they've got a family. They don't want to be out there. And you don't want to be there. You realize you must fire on them or be killed yourself, that's the reality of war. When we took most of the surrendering Iraqis the first day and saw how badly they had been treated and learned that the Republican Guard was behind them, not to back them up, but to make them hold in position, it completely changed your view of the war.

Time: Were you then completely repulsed by the idea of war at that point?

McVeigh: I was taken aback by what I had been told. We all thought we were doing this for your country and these people are terrible, every single one of them. You get over there and you realize two things, they're not so terrible and how is this helping my country?

Time: How many of the enemy did you kill?

McVeigh: There were two. They were firing upon us. I'd like to put that rumor to rest. I think there was one person who either mixed me up with someone else or for some reason was taking a pot shot at me. We rode up within 1600 meters of an enemy position and they fired upon us and we fired back. That was on the second day of the conflict.

Time: How did the war change your outlook on life and your outlook on the military?

McVeigh: It gave me a new perspective on life. First, to value every moment of your life, because it may be your last, you never know. And it opened my eyes to be aware of everything going on around me, to read between the lines of things that I'm told.

II

The [Clinton] administration has said that Iraq has no right to stockpile chemical or biological weapons ("weapons of mass destruction")—mainly because they have used them in the past.

Well, if that's the standard by which these matters are decided, then the U.S. is the nation that set the precedent. The U.S. has stockpiled these same weapons (and more) for over 40 years. The U.S. claims that this was done for deterrent purposes during the "Cold War" with the Soviet Union. Why, then is it invalid for Iraq to claim the same reason (deterrence)—with respect to Iraq's (real) war with, and the continued threat of, its neighbor Iran?

The administration claims that Iraq has used these weapons in the past. We've all seen the pictures that show a Kurdish woman and child frozen in death from the use of chemical weapons. But, have you ever seen these pictures juxtaposed next to pictures from Hiroshima or Nagasaki?

I suggest that one study the histories of World War I, World War II and other "regional conflicts" that the U.S. has been involved in to familiarize themselves with the use of "weapons of mass destruction."

Remember Dresden? How about Hanoi? Tripoli? Baghdad? What about the big ones—Hiroshima and Nagasaki? (At these two locations, the U.S. killed at least 150,000 noncombatants—mostly women and children—in the blink of an eye. Thousands more took hours, days, weeks, or months to die.)

If [Iraqi leader] Saddam [Hussein] is such a demon, and people are calling for war crimes charges and trials against him and his nation, why do we not hear the same cry for blood directed at those responsible for even greater amounts of "mass destruction"—like those responsible and involved in dropping bombs on the cities mentioned above?

The truth is, the U.S. has set the standard when it comes to the stockpiling and use of weapons of mass destruction.

Hypocrisy when it comes to death of children? In Oklahoma City, it was family convenience that explained the presence of a day-care center placed between street level and the law enforcement agencies which occupied the upper floors of the building. Yet when discussion shifts to Iraq, any day-care center in a government building instantly becomes "a shield." Think about that.

(Actually, there is a difference here. The administration has admitted to knowledge of the presence of children in or near Iraqi government buildings, yet they still proceed with their plans to bomb—saying that they cannot be held responsible if children die. There is no such proof, however, that knowledge of the presence of children existed in relation to the Oklahoma City bombing.)

When considering morality and mens rea [criminal intent] in light of these facts, I ask: Who are the true barbarians?

CONTRADICTORY LOGIC

Yet another example of this nation's blatant hypocrisy is revealed by the polls which suggest that this nation is greatly in favor of bombing Iraq.

In this instance, the people of the nation approve of bombing government employees because they are "guilty by association"— they are Iraqi government employees. In regard to the bombing in Oklahoma City, however, such logic is condemned.

What motivates these seemingly contradictory positions? Do people think that government workers in Iraq are any less human than those in Oklahoma City? Do they think that Iraqis don't have families who will grieve and mourn the loss of their loved ones? In this context, do people come to believe that the killing of foreigners is somehow different than the killing of Americans?

I recently read of an arrest in New York City where possession of a mere pipe bomb was charged as possession of a "weapon of mass destruction." If a two pound pipe bomb is a "weapon of mass destruction," then what do people think that a 2,000-pound steel-encased bomb is?

I find it ironic, to say the least, that one of the aircraft that could be used to drop such a bomb on Iraq is dubbed "The Spirit of Oklahoma."

When a U.S. plane or cruise missile is used to bring destruction to a foreign people, this nation rewards the bombers with applause and praise. What a convenient way to absolve these killers of any responsibility for the destruction they leave in their wake.

Unfortunately, the morality of killing is not so superficial. The truth is, the use of a truck, a plane, or a missile for the delivery of a weapon of mass destruction does not alter the nature of the act itself.

These are weapons of mass destruction—and the method of delivery matters little to those on the receiving end of such weapons.

TEACHING BY EXAMPLE

Whether you wish to admit it or not, when you approve, morally, of the bombing of foreign targets by the U.S. military, you are approving of acts morally equivalent to the bombing in Oklahoma City. The only difference is that this nation is not going to see any foreign casualties appear on the cover of *Newsweek* magazine.

It seems ironic and hypocritical that an act viciously condemned in Oklahoma City is now a "justified" response to a problem in a foreign land. Then again, the history of United States policy over the last century, when examined fully, tends to exemplify hypocrisy.

When considering the use of weapons of mass destruction against Iraq as a means to an end, it would be wise to reflect on the words of the late U.S. Supreme Court Justice Louis Brandeis. His words are as true in the context of *Olmstead* [*v. United States* (1928), the first wire-tapping case to reach the Supreme Court, in which Brandeis prophesied that a government unchecked would find more ways to spy on its citizens] as they are when they stand alone: "Our government is the potent, the omnipresent teacher. For good or for ill, it teaches the whole people by its example."

Sincerely, Timothy J. McVeigh

Following the Words
of a Spiritual Master

by Hidetoshi Takahashi, interviewed by Haruki Murakami

In the 1990s, Hidetoshi Takahashi was a member of Aum Shin-rikyo, a Japanese religious cult that combines tenets of Buddhism and other esoteric spiritual doctrines. Twenty-eight-year-old Takahashi was part of Aum in March 1995 when the cult's spiritual guru, Shoko Asahara, prompted several initiates to board Tokyo subway trains and release deadly sarin gas that was carried on board in various containers. According to Takahashi, Asahara's beliefs included an apocalyptic vision of the future, and the terrorist act may have been the leader's attempt to speed that event.

Like most of Aum's members, Takahashi did not take part in the subway gassing; instead he worked in the cult's Ministry of Science and Technology as a subordinate to Hideo Murai, the science minister who helped Asahara attempt to realize his end-of-the-world dreams. In the following interview with author Haruki Murakami, for the book *Underground: The Tokyo Gas Attack and the Japanese Psyche*, Takahashi explains that Asahara used his unique vision of the future to offer salvation to young people. Like Takahashi, many Japanese youths at that time were feeling disillusioned despite the wealth and prosperity of their country. In addition, according to Takahashi, they had already been conditioned by a general feeling in the culture that the closing of the millennium would herald the end of the world. Asahara and Aum Shinrikyo offered a religious alternative to those in need of solace and a sense of belonging in a world on the verge of oblivion.

Over time, Takahashi's faith in the cult began to wane due to his doubts about the integrity of its leadership. His skepticism, he claims, was the main reason why he was not asked to participate in the sarin attacks. Nevertheless, he speaks candidly about how he might have responded had he been confronted with the choice

Hidetoshi Takahashi, "No Matter How Grotesque a Figure Asahara Appears, I Can't Just Dismiss Him," *Underground: The Tokyo Gas Attack and the Japanese Psyche*, by Haruki Murakami, translated by Alfred Birnbaum and Philip Gabriel. London: The Harvill Press, 2000. Copyright © 2000 by Haruki Murakami. Reproduced by permission of International Creative Management, Inc.

of taking part in such a horrendous enterprise. He concludes that those who followed the order to release the gas were under the spell of the cult and got swept up in events and were therefore unable to think logically about what they were doing.

At college I felt a deep alienation between my outer and my inner Self. I was a cheerful, enthusiastic person with lots of friends, but once I was alone in my room, I was engulfed by loneliness and there was nobody I could share that world with. . . .

At high school I was into sports, basketball and badminton, but after entering college I felt I had to draw a line between myself and society. I was what we call a "Moratorium Person": someone who doesn't want to grow up. Our generation grew up after Japan had become a wealthy country and we viewed society through this lens of affluence. I just couldn't adjust to the "adult society" I saw outside. It seemed warped to me somehow. Wasn't there some other way to live your life, some other way of viewing the world? During my college days I had a lot of free time, and was preoccupied with these questions.

When you're young you have all kinds of idealistic notions in your head, but coming face-to-face with the realities of your own life makes you see how immature you are. I felt very frustrated.

To free myself, to make a fresh start, I poked my nose into all sorts of things, hoping to find the energy I needed to live. Life is full of suffering, and the contradictions in the real world irked me. To escape these, I imagined my own sort of utopian society, which made it easier for me to be taken in by a religious group that espoused a similar vision.

When the Aum question comes up, people always start talking about relations between parents and children going sour, and family discord, but it can't be reduced to something so simplistic. Certainly one of the attractions of Aum lay in people's frustrations with reality and unrest in the family, but a much more important factor lies in apocalyptic feelings of "the end of the world", feelings all of us have about the future. If you pay attention to the universal feeling of all of us, all Japanese—all humankind, even—then you can't explain Aum's appeal to so many people by saying it's all based on discord in the family.

Murakami: Hold on a second. You really think all Japanese have a vision of the end of the world?

It might be hard to generalize and say that all of them do, but I think inside all Japanese there is an apocalyptic viewpoint: an invisible, unconscious sense of fear. When I say that all Japanese have this fear I mean some people have already pulled aside the veil, while others have yet to do so. If this veil were suddenly drawn back everyone would feel a sense of terror about the near future, the direction our world's heading in. Society is the foundation stone for people's lives, and they don't know what's going to happen to it in the future. This feeling grows stronger the more affluent a country becomes. It's like a dark shadow looming larger and larger.

Somehow the words "decline" or "collapse" seem to hit the mark more than "the end".

Maybe so, but remember that when I was at school Nostradamus's *Prophecies* became famous, and that sense that "The End Is Nigh" wedged itself deep into my consciousness through the mass media. And I wasn't the only one to feel like that. I don't want this to deteriorate into some simplistic theory about "my generation", but I feel very strongly that all Japanese at that time had the idea drilled into them of 1999 being the end of the world. Aum renunciates have already accepted, inside themselves, the end of the world, because when they become a renunciate, they discard themselves totally, thereby abandoning the world. In other words, Aum is a collection of people who have accepted the end. People who continue to hold out hope for the near future still have an attachment to the world. If you have attachments, you won't discard your Self, but for renunciates it's as if they've leapt right off a cliff. And taking a giant leap like that feels good. They lose something—but gain something in return.

Therefore the idea of "the End" is one of the axes around which Aum Shinrikyo revolved. "Armageddon's coming, so become a renunciate," they urged, "donate all your money to Aum"—and of course that became their source of income. . . .

WHY I CHOSE AUM

Even now there's an element about Aum, its driving force and direction, that I can't fully understand. It had such tremendous energy, and pulled in so many people—including me, of course. But how did it do this?

When I was at college many new religions tried to convert me, but in terms of grappling with the direction the world had taken, seriously formulating a religious world view, searching earnestly for a lifestyle that fitted this view, and then rigorously putting it into practice, Aum stood out head and shoulders above the rest. Aum was the most amazing group of all. I really admired them for the way they practised what they preached. Compared to them, other religions were resigned, cosy, comfortable, passive. Aura training was very, very tough. Their religious view—that you must transform your own body before you can transform the world—had a hardhitting realism. If there's any chance for salvation, I thought, it has to begin like this. . . .

I joined Aum twice. The second time I could already sense the violence that overshadowed Aum. The very first day back I thought: "Uh oh. I've made a big mistake." Aum wore a cheerful mask at the branch offices, since the people there were all still living ordinary lives. But go to Kamikuishiki where it was just renunciates, people who have discarded everything, and you could already feel this urgent sense of desperation.

When I joined I was put to work straight away making Cosmo cleaners. Aum was already claiming that it was being attacked from the outside with sarin gas, and Cosmo cleaners were designed to reduce the toxicity. Just prior to my taking vows the Leader gave a sermon. "I've been hit with poison gas," he told us, coughing and coughing. He was as limp as a rag doll, and his face was all dark. It seemed tremendously real. "I can only last another month," he said, "and at this rate Aum will be destroyed. Before this happens, I want those who believe in me to gather around me. All of you will serve as my shield." It was a powerful sermon. It forced lay followers to question their faith: here is the Leader in such dire straits and you're just sitting around? How can you call this faith? All at once about 300 people took vows, and I was one of them, caught up in this wave. Things started to look strange to me when I was forced to undergo what they called "Christ Initiation". All the followers were made to take drugs. Any way you look at it, the whole thing was carelessly done. Using drugs in the name of religion, in order to enter some elevated state, is suspect in itself, but even supposing you accept it as a legitimate means, at the very least you've got to do it in an organized fashion. What they gave us was something close to LSD, I suspect, and for almost everyone it was their first such experience. Some people went crazy and were just left to their own devices. That really troubled me. Even if the Leader had planned this as a method of elevating our spiritual state, the way it was handled left a lot to be desired.

I felt a great deal of resistance to this whole "Christ Initiation", and after I went through it I struggled with whether or not I should leave Aum. It was such a shock it drove me to tears. "What the hell do they think they're doing?" I wondered. It wasn't just me—even a few of the leadership wavered over this initiation, some of the enlightened practitioners who hung on Asahara's every word. It felt like Aum was starting to fall apart.

I think I joined Aum as a kind of adventure. You have to be a bit forgiving of a system organized to open up an entirely unknown world for you—when in Rome, and all that—so I did accept that system. On the one hand I wanted to adjust to the Aum lifestyle and plunge ahead, while a part of me took a step back and watched it all with a sober eye.

So anyway, after this "Christ Initiation" I had too many doubts about Aum and I couldn't do the work I was assigned. I couldn't easily swallow the doctrine of Vajrayana. There weren't any other followers I could express my doubts to, and the Leader was too high up for me to talk to him directly. Even if I did say to someone I thought Aum was into some questionable things, I'd just get a stereotypical response: "Mr Takahashi, all we can do is follow Aum." I decided I had to talk to one of the leaders if I wanted to get anywhere.

While all this was going on Mr Niimi, Eriko Iida, and Naropa [*Fumihiko Nagura*] asked me to see them, and as another kind of initiation they tied me up and yelled all kinds of things at me: "Why can't you follow the life we lead in Aum?" "You're neglecting your training, aren't you?" "You're not devoted to the Guru!"

Thinking this was a good opportunity, I decided to bring up some of the doubts I'd been having. "Hold on just a second here," I said. "I have a lot of problems with what's going on in our church, and that's why I can't put everything I've got into our activities." I explained what I'd been feeling and Iida said: "We all feel the same way, but the only path for us is to follow the Guru."

I took it a step further: "You don't know all that much about the Guru, so how is it you can follow him? I believe in the Guru, too, but without really knowing who he is, I can't just follow him blindly." No matter how much I pressed them, the answer was always the same: "All we can do is believe him, and follow him.". . .

I don't consider Aum's crimes simply reckless behaviour. Of course part of it was reckless, but there was a religious viewpoint pervading those actions. That's what I want most to learn about. Probably only Asahara and Murai can explain it fully. The other followers were mere pawns, but not these two—they gave the orders, and decided things with a clear vision of their goals. The opponent I was really struggling against, standing up alone to, were the very motives of those two people.

Most of the people arrested in the gas attack were absolutely devoted followers of the Leader who wouldn't let any doubts they might have about Aum stop them from doing exactly as they were told. . . .

If Murai had told you to release the sarin, would you have disobeyed?

I think so, but there's a trick to doing it. The people who carried out the crime were put in a position where they were caught off guard by the orders and couldn't escape. They'd gather in Murai's room and suddenly the leaders would broach the topic, telling them: "This is an order from the top." *An order from the top*—that was like a mantra in Aum. The people who carried out the crime were chosen from among the strongest believers. "You've been specially chosen," they were told. The leaders appealed to their sense of duty. Faith in Aum meant total devotion.

That's why I wasn't chosen to commit the crimes. I was still at the bottom of the heap and hadn't yet reached enlightenment. In other words Aum didn't trust me enough.

There's one thing I don't understand. When I did my interviews with victims of the gas attack, several of them told me that, based on their experience working for companies, if they had been in Aum and been ordered to release the sarin they might well have done it. But you were actually in Aum, yet say you'd have run away from it. Why is that?

Saying I'd run away might be less than honest. If I really search my heart I can say that if Murai had told me to do it, most likely I would have run away. However, if [senior cultist] Yoshihiro Inoue had said to me, "Hidetoshi, this is part of salvation," and passed me the bag with the sarin in it, I would have been very perplexed. If he'd told me to come with him, I might have done so. In other words, it comes down to a question of ties between individuals.

Murai was my boss, but he was cold and too far above me. If he'd told me to do it I would have asked him why, and if he'd insisted and said, "It's a dirty job but it's for the sake of Aum and I really want you to do it," I like to think that I would have hidden my true feelings, said okay, and then, at the last minute, found a way to get out of it. Like [Ken'ichi] Hirose, who wavered and got off the train, I think I would have struggled over what I should do, but in the end would have found a way out.

But something about Inoue captivated me. He felt a strong sense of religious duty. If I'd seen him agonizing over the situation, I think I would have done anything to help out. He was a great influence on me. So if he'd pushed me saying this was a mission only we could carry out, I might very well have gone along. I would have been operating on a different plane. What I mean is, in the final analysis, logic doesn't play a strong role in people's motivations. I doubt if the ones who did it were even capable of thinking logically when they were given the order to release the sarin. They didn't have the presence of mind, got caught up in events, panicked, and did what they were told. No one who had the strength to think logically about it would have carried it out. In extreme cases of guruism individuals' value systems are completely wiped out. In situations like that people just don't have the mental stamina to connect their actions with the deaths of many people.

No matter how much you resist and try to put a stop to things, the fact is that in a group like Aum your sense of Self steadily deteriorates. Things are forced on you from above and you're continually attacked for not accepting the status quo, not being devoted enough, and inevitably your spirit is broken. I was somehow able to hold out, but a lot of people who entered at the same time ended up broken.

All right, but what if Shoko Asahara himself ordered you— "Takahashi, I want you to do it,"—what would you have done?

I think I would have stood up to him. If he'd been able to give me a reasonable explanation, I would have listened. But if he couldn't, I would have kept asking questions until I was convinced. That alone would have excluded me from the job. I'd spoken my mind in front of him before, and he'd told me I'm a very straightforward type of person. I don't think either Shoko Asahara or Hideo Murai would have been able to move me because they never opened up to me. . . .

I'd like to ask you once more about the idea of the end of the world. Is the Apocalypse that Aum talks about the same as that of Judaism and Christianity? The idea of the millennium is a Western concept, after all, and Nostradamus has nothing to do with Buddhism.

No matter what special spin Aum might put on its idea of Armageddon, I don't think it can compete with the Christian idea of the Apocalypse. It's absorbed into the Christian idea. That's why you can't really explain these Aum-related incidents by looking only at the core of what makes up Aum—namely, Buddhism and Tibetan esoteric religion.

Earlier I said that I don't think that an apocalyptic vision is confined to myself as an individual; what I meant was that, whether you're Christian or not, we all inevitably bear the same apocalyptic fate.

To tell the truth, I don't really understand what you've been calling an apocalyptic vision. But I have the feeling that, if that vision is to have any kind of meaning at all, it has to lie in how you internally deconstruct it.

You're absolutely right. Apocalypse is not some set idea, but more of a process. After an apocalyptic vision there's always a purging or purifying process that takes place. In this sense I think the gas attack was a kind of catharsis, a psychological release of everything that had built up in Japan—the malice, the distorted consciousness we have. Not that the Aum incident got rid of everything. There's still this suppressed, virus-like apocalyptic vision that's invading society and hasn't been erased or digested.

Even if you could get rid of it at an individual level, the virus would remain on a social level.

You talk about society as a whole, but in the so-called secular world, ordinary people—by which I mean people who maintain a relative balance in their lives—deconstruct that kind of virus-like apocalyptic vision, as you put it, in their own way, and naturally substitute something else for it. Don't you think so?

Yes, it does come down to a process of deconstruction. Something like that has absolutely got to take place. Shoko Asahara couldn't deconstruct it, and lost out to apocalyptic ideas. And that's why he had to create a crisis on his own. The apocalyptic vision of Shoko Asahara—as a religious figure—was defeated by an even greater vision.

I've been trying hard to come to terms with these Aum-related incidents. I go to the trial as often as I can. But when I see and hear Asahara at the trial I feel as though he's making an idiot out of me. I get nauseous, and actually vomited once. It's a sad and dreary feeling. Sometimes I think it's not worth watching, but I still can't take my eyes off him. No matter how grotesque a figure Asahara appears, I can't just dismiss him. We should never forget that, if even for a short time, this person named Shoko Asahara functioned in the world and brought about these tragic events. Unless I overcome the "Aum Shinrikyo Incident" inside me, I'll never be able to move on.

Witnesses and Survivors
of Terrorist Actions

Helping Other Passengers During the Tokyo Subway Gas Attacks

by Naoyuki Ogata

On March 20, 1995, members of Japan's Aum Shinrikyo cult contaminated several crowded Tokyo subway trains with lethal sarin gas. A dozen people died from exposure to the gas and five thousand others suffered less-fatal symptoms in the wake of the attacks. The gas was hidden in everyday objects, such as a soda can and a briefcase, that the cultists secreted on the trains. Unsuspecting victims were unaware of their exposure to the sarin gas until well after the gas was released.

Naoyuki Ogata was a twenty-eight-year-old software maintenance technician working in the Tokyo neighborhood of Roppongi at the time of the attacks. Commuting on Tokyo's public transportation system was an everyday necessity for him and millions of others. On Monday, March 20, Ogata was riding a train on the Hibiya Line en route to his job when an intercom announcement stated that the train would not continue into the city. Deciding to take a taxi the rest of the way, Ogata headed toward street level where he was confronted with the nightmarish scene of people dropping to the ground and convulsing due to exposure to the sarin gas.

Ogata, in the following narrative, details his role in organizing a small-scale rescue effort. He assisted several victims at street level and then went back down to the train platform to help a debilitated station attendant. By this point, he had been exposed to a large amount of the gas and began to feel its effects. He finally gave in and followed others to the hospital for treatment.

Ogata concludes his narrative by venting his anger about the lack of municipal assistance during the emergency. Tokyo police, he says, were unorganized and of little help, and only one ambulance arrived on the scene after half an hour of waiting.

Naoyuki Ogata, "We'll Never Make It. If We Wait for the Ambulance We're Done For," *Underground: The Tokyo Gas Attack and the Japanese Psyche*, by Haruki Murakami, translated by Alfred Birnbaum and Philip Gabriel. London: The Harvill Press, 2000. Copyright © 2000 by Haruki Murakami. Reproduced by permission of International Creative Management, Inc.

My company's in Roppongi. I catch the bus around 7.00 to Gotanno Station, then take the 7.42 or 7.47 Hibiya Line train for Naka-meguro. It's incredibly packed. Sometimes you can't even get on. Crowded as it is, though, even more people squeeze in at Kita-senju. You're just squashed in like the filling in a sandwich. I'm talking physical harm. You feel like you'll be crushed to death, or suddenly your hip's thrown out of joint. You're all twisted out of shape and all you can think is "It hurts!" You're just mangled up in the middle of all this, with only your feet in the same place.

It's quite literally a pain to commute like that every day. Come Monday morning I always think "Maybe I won't go in today . . ." (*laughs*) But you know, even though your head's saying "No way, I don't want to go!", your body just automatically sets off for the office. . . .

ON THE WAY TO WORK

On 20 March I missed several trains because they were delayed due to fog on the Toné River. I ended up catching the 7.50-something, which, because of the delay, was packed tight. It was terrible. The previous Friday I'd come down with a cold and had a temperature, so I'd taken the day off. But I was back on the job on Saturday. I had to change over a system for a customer. I took Sunday off and slept the whole day. On Monday I was still a bit out of it; I really wanted to take the day off, but I'd already told my boss I'd go in.

Quite a few people got off at Ueno Station, so finally I could breathe. I'd somehow held onto a handstrap. What do I do while I'm on the subway? Nothing. I'm just thinking, "Gaah, I want to sit down!" (*laughs*).

That day the train stopped between Akihabara and Kodemma-cho. Then there was an announcement about an explosion at Tsuk-iji. "The train will be stopping at Kodemmacho," it said. "Shit," I thought, "first the fog, now this accident. It's just not my day." I was already seriously late.

The train stopped just that once, then went on to Kodemmacho. I was certain it would start again sooner or later, so I waited on board. But not long afterwards there was another announcement: "This train is stopping here. We do not foresee moving on again." What could I do but get off? I decided to take a taxi the rest of the way to the office. So I walked up the stairs to the ticket barrier and went above ground. Suddenly I met with the most amazing sight.

People were dropping like flies all over the place.

I'd taken the third carriage from the back and had absolutely no idea what was happening at the front of the platform. I was just heading up above ground, swearing under my breath like everyone else, when right before my eyes I see three people fall down and foam at the mouth, their arms and legs twitching. "What the hell's going on here?" I thought.

Closest to me was this man whose limbs were quivering, he was trembling all over and foaming at the mouth, having some kind of seizure. I just looked at him and my jaw dropped. I knew it was serious and rushed over to ask him what had happened. I could see he needed immediate care. That's when someone who was still walking by said, "Him foaming like that is dangerous, you'd better stuff some newspaper in his mouth." So we both helped him. After that all these exhausted people kept coming up from the ticket barrier below, then dropping to the floor. I couldn't work out what had happened. Some of the people sitting down suddenly just keeled over flat out.

THE SMALL-SCALE RESCUE EFFORT BEGINS

It was a strange sight. Off towards the back of the next building, this old man—I mean really old—wasn't breathing and there was no pulse. He'd gone motionless just where he lay. "Did anyone call an ambulance?" I asked the person nearest me. "They called," he said, "but none came." Then somebody else said: "We'll never make it. If we wait for the ambulance we're done for." We decided we had to try stopping cars and asking the drivers to help move everyone out.

The traffic light had just turned red, so we all jumped in front of the cars and begged them: "Please, you have to take us to St Luke's." That was the nearest hospital. We went for vans mostly, thinking they could carry five or six people. Everyone stopped for us, and once we'd explained the situation they were understanding and took us.

I must have been doing that for an hour, helping carry across those who'd dragged themselves up above ground. We passed them along like a relay team. We divided ourselves up between the "people-carriers" and the "car-stoppers".

The ambulances just didn't come. Finally one ambulance did show up, but only after about half an hour. It had come from miles away because all the others were at Tsukiji. One ambulance!

I went to the hospital by taxi, too. I'd been so busy helping people, by the time I'd finished I was showing symptoms myself. The main reason was I'd gone back down to the platform. Word was that a station attendant had collapsed and another attendant came up saying, "Can anyone give me a hand?" So I went down again together with a few others and breathed in the sarin. By that time the station was full of gas. . . .

The fallen station attendant was barely conscious and muttering something about, "No, no, I have to remain here in the station." He'd somehow leaned against the ticket barrier and still he was saying, "I have to stay here." We had to drag him out of there by force.

I didn't think twice about going down to the platform. Scared or not, I wasn't even aware of it; we were too desperate. All I knew was we had to help. There were only a handful of people still on their feet, how could we not help? Going back down, there was a paint-thinner-like smell. I remember thinking, "Odd, who dimmed the lights?" My pupils were contracted.

A MUCH-NEEDED HOSPITAL VISIT

After we'd carried out all the injured and got our breath back, I was trying to get a taxi to work when I started to feel sick. My head hurt, I felt nauseous, my eyes itched. The others told me, "If you're feeling strange you'd better go to the hospital."

Three of us shared a taxi. One guy had come up from Osaka or Nagoya on business, and he was grumbling: "Why did this have to happen today? I just got here." I sat in the front seat; the two men in the back were pretty dizzy, so we wound down the windows all the way. The roads were jammed. Tsukiji was sealed off and there was no way of getting to any backstreets, so we had to head straight down Harumi Avenue which was packed, a real mess.

They tested my eyes at the hospital and put me on a drip straight away. The place seemed like a combat hospital, IV drips lining the corridors. . . . I got two drips, then, since my symptoms weren't so bad at the time, I went home. The doctor even asked me "Are you going home or staying?" but I was so worked up, as if I'd just left a war zone, I didn't even notice if I was tired or weak or anything.

By the time I got home my eyes really hurt. I could barely sleep for a week. I'd shut my eyes, but they still hurt—the whole night through until morning . . . that wore me out. So I went back to the hospital for more tests and was told my cholinesterase level was way down and I was showing the effects of sarin. I wish they'd told me earlier. Ever since the Matsumoto incident they knew what the symptoms of sarin were and they must have had testing procedures. And St Luke's is one of the better places. Most of the other hospitals were so poorly equipped it was a joke. . . .

CRITIQUE OF TOKYO'S EMERGENCY RESPONSE SYSTEM

To tell the truth, though, I have my doubts about the Police and Fire department. Okay they sprang into action in the beginning at Tsukiji, but even so they were just way too late in coming to help at Kodemmacho. We'd given up on them by the time they arrived. I just wonder what would have happened if we hadn't taken it upon ourselves to do something. Granted the local police might not have any experience, but they were practically useless. Ask them which hospital to go to, and that hasn't been established so they're on the radio for ten minutes. Just a simple question: "Which hospital?"

The police only showed up after the rescue operation was practically over. Then they began directing traffic for the one ambulance that arrived. I don't know what's wrong with Japan's standby disaster arrangements. After all those sarin gas victims in Matsumoto, they ought to have learned a lesson or two. They'd identified a link between Aum and sarin at that time. If they'd followed that up this whole gas attack wouldn't have happened, or at least I'd have come away with less serious injuries.

At the hospital I saw some of the others who had helped me rescue people from Kodemmacho Station. Some were bedridden. We all inhaled sarin. I don't want to keep quiet about this thing; keeping quiet is a bad Japanese habit. By now, I know everyone's beginning to forget about this whole incident, but I absolutely do not want people to forget.

Rising Above the Tragedy of the Oklahoma City Bombing

by Richard Williams

On April 19, 1995, Timothy McVeigh detonated a homemade bomb inside a van parked outside the Murrah Federal Building in Oklahoma City, Oklahoma. McVeigh was a former U.S. Army sergeant who had served in Operation Desert Storm in 1991. Following his army service, McVeigh had become disillusioned with the U.S. government and had become interested in extreme right-wing ideology. He was especially upset about federal law enforcement actions in Ruby Ridge, Idaho, in 1992 and Waco, Texas, in 1993, both of which resulted in the loss of citizens' lives. The bombing of the Murrah building, which housed federal law enforcement offices, was believed to be retaliation for these events—particularly the Waco tragedy. The blast killed 168 people, including federal employees, children, and tourists.

Richard Williams, an employee charged with maintaining the federal building, survived the explosion. He suffered extensive injuries as a result of the bombing, including lacerations, a fractured skull, a severed ear, and a crushed right hand. In the following article, Williams recounts his experience that day and his recovery period that followed. He also discusses his involvement in designing the memorial that commemorates the tragedy. Williams's recollections were taken down in an interview with Al Siebert, the coordinator of the Survivor Guidelines Web site from which this article was taken.

At 9:02 A.M. on April 19th, 1995, the people . . . in the Murrah Building were just like you—employees or visitors there to do business with various agencies. There were children entrusted to the daycare where they could be near their parents, delivery people, and people parking in the lot across the street. It was like any other day.

No distinction was made by the bomb or its makers. The only thing we had in common was our innocence. There were 168 deaths. 118 were federal workers, 19 children, 1 rescue worker, 26 visitors, 3 in buildings across the street to the north, and 1 outside near the blast. In my . . . office, we lost two friends and employees, Mike Loudenslager and Steve Curry. In all, 426 persons were treated in area hospitals. Over 300 surrounding buildings still bear scars from that day. Many remain uninhabited. Boarded up windows are a common sight in the area and a constant reminder.

BEFORE THE BOMB

My office was on the first floor in the west end of the building. The sidewalk and 5th street were only a few feet from my office window on the north. I had started my day as I usually did about 6:30 A.M. coming in early to beat the traffic and get caught up on memos and other administrative things required of me as Principal Assistant Manager. Around 9:00 o'clock I had just left a meeting with some of my staff in the office behind me and was standing talking in my office with my planner estimator. Little did we know that at the same time, less than 100 feet to the east of me was a Ryder truck parking in front of the building. That truck and its contents changed us for the rest of our lives.

AFTER THE BOMB EXPLODED

Much of what happened is still a puzzle for me. Even today some of the pieces haven't been put back together. I stirred to consciousness lying on my side and noticed my arm with a pink shirt sleeve covered with blood. I was dazed, in shock and confused. I thought I must be in a dream. I felt, heard, and saw nothing until I began to come to. Then I heard someone screaming nearby and a voice I thought was directed at me saying, "hold on, I'll be right back." I began to ask for help, and though several of my coworkers heard me, they couldn't get to me. One of my co-workers, Dot Hill, says she was even walking on the debris which was on top of me and didn't know it. Shortly after the voice told me to hang on, I felt someone pulling the pieces of the building off of me. All I could see was this massive torso of a man and could feel him lifting me up like a baby to carry me out to a waiting ambulance. I tried to walk, but couldn't and didn't understand why. My coworker and friend Tom Hall and I were put in the same ambulance and taken to the hospital. The man who got us out was OKC police officer Terry Yeakey, a gentle giant who had a hard time with the "hero" label he was given after the bombing. In fact, he took his own life the following year. The answers to many of my questions died with him because only he knew the exact details of my rescue. Many rescuers and survivors are tormented by the events of that day and the days and weeks that followed.

I was given emergency treatment (triage) in the Labor and Delivery section of the hospital. Thank goodness no babies were being born at that time! I had the full attention of the staff there along with the eye and ear specialists, the orthopedic surgeon, and the general surgeon who'd been called to care for me. A few weeks later I got a great card from the Labor and Delivery staff who hailed me as their first male patient! They also told me I needed to learn how to push better. . . .

My family kept the full impact of what had happened from me until the next morning when the medication had worn off and I was more coherent. I really didn't understand the extent of the damage to the Murrah Building until Friday. When I saw the first pictures of the building on television, I immediately asked about the children, my coworkers, and the friends who'd been a part of my life for the past 20 years. I still didn't totally comprehend the impact this event would have on the world.

RECOVERY

The days that followed are pretty much a blur. My wife Lynne talks about the nurse trying to comb the glass out of my hair missing the 20 staples which held my scalp together. According to her, it looked like I had glitter in my hair from the thousands of tiny fragments of glass. Over the ensuing weeks, I had 2-3 doctor appointments each week. My crushed right hand required two surgeries, the ear specialist had to remove glass from my ear canal on more than one occasion—including a large piece which had lodged in the eardrum itself. Regular visits to physical therapy lasted 18 months. The plastic surgeon removed a large piece of glass from my cheek in July of '95. Pieces of glass still work their way to the surface and have to be removed. They are constant reminders of how fortunate I have been to have survived. With my wife Lynne as my chauffeur, I returned to work for a few hours a day only 43 days after the bombing. . . .

Knowing the building as I did as a maintenance, mechanic, mechanic foreman, and buildings manager, I don't think any other building could have withstood such a blast without greater loss of life. It was built of reinforced concrete and treated with fire resistant materials. It was certainly difficult to see it imploded on May 23, 1995.

I was fortunate enough to help draft and get approved a Mission Statement which was to become the cornerstone in shaping and guiding the design and development of the memorial. It represents a remarkable community consensus document which evolved under the most difficult of circumstances. The process of developing this Memorial so soon after a tragedy of this magnitude is unprecedented. After an eight month massive input campaign from families, survivors, community members, and more than 10,000 people across the world in March of 1996, the Memorial Task Force unanimously approved the Memorial Mission Statement. . . .

In October of 1997, President Clinton signed Public Law 105-58 establishing the OKC National Memorial as a unit of the National Parks Service and designating the OKC National Memorial Trust

I was honored when President Clinton named me as one of the nine members of the trust and recall with gratitude his endorsement of the Oklahoma City National Memorial at a ceremony at the White House in August, 1998. To say that this was an experience of a lifetime is an incredible understatement.

Tragedies like this just doesn't happen in the United States, especially in a place like Oklahoma. The horror of what occurred will stay with us always, but also will the courage and determination and love displayed by people from everywhere and all walks of life. It's our hope that the memorial will speak to the pain and the healing as the Mission statement so simply suggests:

> We Come Here to Remember Those Who Were Killed, Those
> Who Survived, and Those Changed Forever. May All Who
> Leave Here Know the Impact of Violence. May This Memorial
> Offer Comfort, Strength, Peace, Hope and Serenity.

Losing a Sister in the Kenyan Bombing

by Mellina Fanouris

On the morning of Friday, August 7, 1998, Muslim extremists, who were part of Osama bin Laden's al Qaeda terrorist network, detonated two bombs that destroyed two U.S. embassies in Africa—the first in Nairobi, Kenya, and moments later, a second in Tanzania's capital, Dar es Salaam. The blast from the Nairobi bomb, comprised of 800kg of TNT, sent out a shockwave that was felt 6 miles from the center of the city. The immediate, 150-meter radius of destruction claimed 260 lives. The death toll, compounded with 5,000 injured, created an emergency crisis for authorities in Nairobi.

Phaedra Vrontamitis, a Greek citizen employed by the embassy as a personnel specialist, was among the casualties that day in Nairobi. Mellina Fanouris, Phaedra's sister, lived and worked in Nairobi, as did several members of their family. In her book entitled *Phaedra*, from which the following narrative was taken, Fanouris describes her reaction upon learning of the attack and the eventual death of her beloved sibling.

Fanouris relates that she was in her office in Gigiri, a neighborhood ten kilometers (about six miles) from the center of Nairobi, when the bomb exploded. She tells of hearing that the explosion had originated at the embassy where her sister was working and of the trials of her husband who rushed to the scene to aid in the rescue effort. Sadly, the hopes and prayers of the entire family came to naught when they learned of the tragic fate of their beloved Phae.

Inside the five-story building of the U.S. Embassy, the morning began as a normal day with staff finishing the week's work and looking forward to a well deserved weekend. Oblivious to the fact that their lives would be altered forever, everyone was busy replying to e-mails and taking action on matters that couldn't wait until Monday. . . .

THE BOMB IS DETONATED

At 10.37 A.M. a loud explosion muffled the noise of traffic, leading many employees to rush to their windows to see what was its cause. Before anyone had a chance to actually fathom what was going on, a second, deafening blast followed. Outside, in the rear parking lot, terrorists had detonated a vehicle packed with hundreds of pounds of explosives. The explosion tore with incredible force through the rear side of the Embassy. The blast instantaneously killed most occupants of the first three floors facing the back of the building.

Outside, a hellish scene unfolded. The damage inflicted on pedestrians and bystanders was devastating. Innocent lives were shattered for ever. The eight-story Ufundi House building, immediately adjacent to the back of the chancery, looked like a giant sand pit made of chunks and slabs of concrete.

Shock waves of the blast were felt at our offices in Gigiri—ten kilometers [about six miles] away from the city center.

ANXIETY SETS IN

The phone in my office rang and I hastened to pick it up. Before I had a chance to place the receiver to my ear, [my close friend] Brigitte's question sent a chill up my spine.

"Is Phae all right?" she asked, her voice trembling with anxiety. I felt the blood drain from my body as one of my closest friends explained what had taken place. A scream died in my throat.

Like a zombie, unable to control my shaking fingers, I dialed Phae's number. My heart was thumping so loudly, my ears hurt. "Please pick up," I begged. "Please tell me you're okay." My efforts were futile. The phone lines were all jammed. From the adjoining office, a colleague switched on her radio. There we heard the blood curdling announcement. The extent of loss of life and injuries was horrendous—hospitals were imploring for blood donors and blankets.

The phones in our office began ringing simultaneously. My colleagues were running from one desk to the next. The news had spread like wildfire.

THE FAMILY RESPONDS

"I've just heard," [my brother] Laki's voice was trembling. "I'm driving straight to the Embassy."

49

Before Laki had even turned on the ignition, Muiruri [the household cook] had opened the door and jumped in.

"*Haya, twende,* my friend," he yelled, pointing his hand towards the city center. There was gravity in his voice, urging Laki to hurry. Muiruri had followed his childhood buddy from the time they were young boys to adulthood. He was there when Laki got married, when the children were born, and now as tragedy struck, he was beside him.

As they reached the outskirts of the city center, they found people running in all directions away from the shattering glass and flying debris.

"Mellina," it was [my husband] Lukas. "I'm rushing over to Phae. Try and stay calm."

"Can you see what is happening from your office?" I asked.

"Clouds of dark smoke," he replied. "I have to go. Will call you as soon as I can."

The Greek Embassy was situated on the 13th floor of Nation Centre. From Lukas' window he could see much more than he wanted to admit. Without losing any time, he raced down the stairs and kept running until he reached the calamitous site.

"Have you heard from Mum?" [Phae's sons] Leon and Paulie were ringing from England, [her son] Alexi from Australia—the boys were crushed. There was little I could tell them that would lessen the blow. . . .

ARRIVING ON THE SCENE

When Laki and Muiruri reached the site of the devastation, Lukas was already there, minutes after the Marines had established a security perimeter cordoning off the site.

Stopping for just a few seconds to get his breath back, Laki approached one of the Marines that was standing on guard. "My sister . . . , Phae . . . , is . . . inside," he said, his voice breaking up while he tried to get his breath back. "Let me go to her."

"I'm sorry, sir," he replied tightening his grip on the machine gun he was holding. "I understand your predicament, but we can't allow anyone near the building. There could be another terrorist attack. For your own safety," he pointed at the three men in front of him, "I suggest you move away."

"Who cares about *our* safety," Lukas and Laki answered in unison.

"She could be hurt. We need to help her," Laki persisted, moving closer.

"If you take one more step, sir," the Marine threatened, "I'll have to shoot you."

"Let's grab some of those gloves that they are distributing," Lukas turned to Laki, "and assist the injured. Maybe some good samaritan will do the same for Phae."

At 6.00 P.M. I was still stuck at my desk waiting for news. Finally, Laki called. "We have been to every hospital in town. We tried calling the emergency numbers issued by the Americans. The information they have given us is that Phae is listed as missing." He sighed heavily. "Lukas suggests we all meet at home, regroup and start doing the rounds of hospitals and clinics again."

THE NIGHTMARE IS CONFIRMED

Out at Rosslyn, our mother was in a terrible state. It was as if she had been struck by lightning. The youngsters had not been able to prevent her from watching the news, and the whole destruction had unfolded before her eyes.

"I'm not going to lose hope," she said, looking up with fear in her eyes.

While we were deciding who was going to go where, we heard a car drive in. For a split second, my hopes were raised. Someone was bringing Phae home. We made a dash for the main door. We saw people getting out of the car and coming towards us. I recognized two of Phae's colleagues from the Embassy, the First Secretary of the Greek Embassy and Rose Sideras—a family friend. The expression on their faces said it all. Our worst nightmare was confirmed.

Phae had died as she had lived. She was found among the rubble of her office protecting Hindu with her body. Hindu was one of the youngest staff members whom Phae had taken under her wing. She was five months pregnant.

Duty First During the 9/11 Attack on the Pentagon

by Janet Deltuva

On September 11, 2001, terrorists working for the al Qaeda network staged attacks against the United States by hijacking domestic airliners and using them as missiles to strike select targets. Four planes were seized in the operation, one of which failed to reach its objective. Of the three other aircraft, two struck the World Trade Center in New York, and the final plane was guided into the Pentagon in Washington, D.C. The latter aircraft, American Airlines Flight 77, crashed into the Pentagon's helicopter pad on the western side of the building at 9:38 A.M. The resulting explosion caused extensive damage to a section of the complex that housed offices for the U.S. Marine Corps. Reports from the U.S. Department of Defense state that 125 employees, service members, and contract workers, as well as the 64 passengers aboard Flight 77, were killed in the attack.

Janet Deltuva was an air force major employed as a biomedical sciences corps specialist in the Pentagon. Like many people that day, she was in no way prepared for the bedlam that followed the attack. In the following article, an excerpt from Dean E. Murphy's *September 11: An Oral History*, Deltuva gives an account of her initial reaction to the explosion and her attempt to maintain a level head during the chaotic emergency response. Her military training, Deltuva claims, allowed her to function with detachment during the harrowing rescue effort.

I thought it was an accident when I saw what had happened at the Twin Towers. I was preparing for a trip to Texas when someone in the office got a telephone call. A plane had struck the World Trade Center. About fifteen of us got up and walked to the boss's office, where there is a television. A lot of these guys I work with are pilots and know a lot about planes. "Do you think it is a navigational error?" I asked. "Come on, Janet, that is not a navigational error!" one of them shot back. "Maybe it's an air traffic control problem," I suggested. "Get real," another one of them said. "It's terrorism." People were coming and going from the office. I wanted to hear the president so I stayed behind to watch as the others called colleagues in the building. My boss, Colonel Guy Dahlbeck, came in with his gym bag and placed it in his office chair.

"What's going on?" he asked.

"Two planes hit the World Trade Center," one of the pilots told him. "What a target DC is—the White House or the Pentagon," I said to no one in particular.

THE PLANE HITS

Just then there was a loud screeching sound and WHUMP! The screeching was the plane engine accelerating and the "whump" was the plane hitting the Pentagon. We are in the flight pattern for Reagan Airport, so we hear planes all of the time, but this was different. Everybody just knew something big had happened. We all started running. I got back to my office shouting, "Let's go! Let's go!" Someone asked me, "Do you really think we need to go?" Then the fire alarms sounded. Finally he agreed it was necessary for us to leave. My friend who sits behind me, Lt. Col. Maureen Massey, was taking her time. I think she was in shock and denial for a minute. She asked me if she should take her purse. She wanted to make a phone call. I started demanding that we needed to get going. She asked, "Should I take my lunch?" Finally I told her that I was leaving with or without her and started toward the door. Maureen followed quickly. As we were rushing out of the building, Maureen started to cry. "You can't cry," I told her. "You need to get out of here." She started to worry about the children in the day-care center where her daughter had once attended. That really made her upset. "You can't panic," I told her. "You need to walk out of here. You need to be calm. If you lose it, it will cause a chain reaction."

I put my hand around her shoulder and we left. People were scrambling toward the exits all over. As we were leaving our work center we looked all around to be sure our officemates were leaving with us, but no one wanted to linger behind too long. As we went down the staircase, I could see the black smoke and deep fire across the way. I thought it might be a bomb. People were saying it was an airplane, but I didn't know how they knew that. There was an announcement on the overhead speaker directing us away from the corridors closest to the impact of the plane. As we walked out of the building, many of us hugged and reassured each other. The route we took was right by the medical clinic. I am a biomedical sciences corps specialist and had received disaster preparedness training, so I decided to stop at the clinic. I am not a doctor, so I knew I would not be saving lives directly, but I could organize and assist and serve as a gofer.

I told Maureen to keep moving and to find a safe spot. But she wanted to stay. "If you are going to be a basket case, you can't come," I remember saying. She said she was okay, and as it turned out, she was really a great help. . . .

When I went into the clinic, everyone was already in full gear doing what they had been trained to do—and all branches of the service were working together. Someone said, "I need this to go to the center courtyard." It was a large silver case full of medical supplies. I grabbed it and ran. At that point, I was very thankful that I had not worn a skirt or heels that day.

When I got to the courtyard, the scene was horrible. There were people gasping for air because their lungs were choked with smoke. Some people had burns and others were in shock. One man was in particularly bad shape, his burned skin hanging off him like gray confetti. I scrambled to look for supplies as the doctors and nurses rendered care. "I need an IV line! I need oxygen! I need tape!" Sometimes what they asked for was available, and sometimes it was not. Army nurse Major Laurie Brown had a radio and she called back to the clinic when we couldn't come up with something needed. Triage areas were set up in the courtyard. Someone was yelling, "Expectant to the left. Immediate to the right and walking wounded over there!"

REMAINING CALM AMIDST THE CHAOS

At the beginning of all this I prayed. "Jesus, help me know what to do and not get in the way." That was crucial. I wanted to help but I did not want to cause a problem. Most of the time, I felt very calm and was assured that I was doing some good. But I had my moments of fear too. I don't think I wanted to admit I was scared, but I know I must have been. Initially when I called my husband I got his voice mail and left a message. I listened to it later and my voice on the recording sounded scared. Once I walked to the bathroom feeling so overwhelmed that I cried the whole way. When I got there, I stopped so people wouldn't see me. And then I cried all the way back, stopping again just in time. I just knew I couldn't give in.

Sometimes I looked at people, and I could see that they might break down, but we would both look away before that could happen. If you started crying, the fear was that you wouldn't be able to stop. There is no life experience that prepared me for this. When I underwent emergency readiness training, we pretended a plane had crashed. We pretended to have noise and smoke. We pretended to crawl under barbed wire. And we pretended to load stretchers on a plane. Maybe some of the day I was doing some of that pretending—pretending that it was an exercise. I guess that is why the military trains so much, so that everything is surreal and almost automatic so you can get through it when you really need to.

I am a stickler for detail, so I paid attention to many of the seemingly little things. I kept reminding people to drink water so that they wouldn't become dehydrated. I also gathered pieces of debris that had fallen in the courtyard and put them under the benches so that people wouldn't trip on them. When people picked up a piece as a souvenir, I scolded them. "That is evidence!" I shouted. Later in the day, I got a pair of sneakers from my car and gave them to a woman wearing high heels. I also distributed surgical gloves to everyone and nagged them to keep them on. For some, I think it was an annoyance. Lt. General Paul Carlton, the Air Force surgeon general, was involved in the rescue effort. I kept giving him gloves and he kept ditching them. Once when he emerged from the building he was sooty and had what appeared to be molten metal on the back of his physician's vest. I handed him a towel, a surgical mask and some more gloves. He chuckled when he saw the gloves. "You don't understand," he said. I guess he was there for a far greater purpose, and universal medical precautions were not a priority—saving lives was.

ASSISTING IN THE RESCUE EFFORT

A Navy enlisted lady came out of the building stumbling with some folks supporting her as she fell to the grass. Her name was Christine and she was having trouble breathing. She lay on the ground with tears rolling on her face. I went over to reassure her and the chaplain came to my side. Knowing that she was okay, I looked around again for someone else in need of help. A lieutenant colonel from the Army walked out of the building and was insisting that he was all right. He was wet and his eyebrows and eyelashes were singed. "Sit down," I said to him. He ignored me. "Sit down," I insisted. He got angry with me. "Major, you are not going to tell me when to sit down," he said. But it was too late. Two nurses grabbed him, sat him on the ground, stuck a needle in his arm and started an IV. When he calmed down a bit, he said that he had been standing in his office talking to someone when suddenly the floor pushed up from under them. He fell, but managed to get up and run to safety.

I couldn't keep track of time, but at some point we heard that there were two more hijacked planes inbound and that we needed to clear the area. I looked around and grabbed some supplies. There was an Army lieutenant colonel in a dirtied uniform who was struggling to support a civilian woman with her arm bandaged. I ran over and helped him with her. As we approached the Pentagon—we were going to cut through the building and get out the other side—a patient on a stretcher was screaming not to go back inside. They tried to calm her and pressed forward. The lady I was helping was becoming weaker and I was having difficulty holding her. A man saw me struggling and took over. By the end of the day, my body ached so much it felt like a truck ran over me.

We relocated outside the Pentagon. Things were more organized there, with people writing triage tags on the patients. I asked one young man there named John if he would like to call his family on my cell phone to let them know that he was safe. He asked me to call his mother, Georgia, who lives in Niagara Falls, near where I grew up in Cheektowaga, New York. As I was dialing, he asked to take the phone. "Let me talk to her," he said. "If she hears your voice you'll scare her." Just then there was the loud thundering sound of fighter jets overhead. Several victims were traumatized by the airplane sound and we had to reassure them that it was our own. "It's our boys," I said. "It's the good guys." I couldn't get through to John's mother before he was taken to the hospital, but I kept trying afterward. When I finally reached her, I started the conversation abruptly, "John is okay," I said before even identifying myself. She cried and thanked me many times over for calling.

Next I went over to a lady covered with a blanket, bundled on a stretcher. She was a civilian. The head of her stretcher was on the down slope of a small hill with her feet at the top, probably to help with the shock. She was alone and I went over to her to reassure her. Her name was Pat, and she had a very rough voice from the smoke inhalation. I asked if she wanted me to call someone for her, but she said no. She asked for her purse and described it as a black bag with two handles. I laughed a little and hoped she would too when I said, "We all have black bags in the military." I never did find her bag.

Soon after that I was told to move over to the south parking lot, where a medical station was being set up. This was the hub. It was directly in front of the impact area from the plane. Medical personnel were putting up tents and supplies were pouring in. I stood waiting for directions. A captain from the Navy asked for someone who could take notes, so I raised my hand and volunteered. I was going to be his runner. I soon learned that his name was John Feerick, a reserve neurologist from Ohio. His office for reserve duty was destroyed by the plane. Had he not gone to buy some T-shirts for his kids, he would have been killed. I scrambled to find something to write on, and the only paper I could find was an FBI evidence bag. The FBI guy looked at me. Our eyes met. I just grabbed the bag and acted like I belonged there.

At this point, they were still expecting many survivors to be pulled from inside but no one could get into the building until the fire was under control. While we waited, one of my assignments was to find two volunteers who could identify "living and dead" for triage. I found them and also called Walter Reed Medical Center to determine how many beds were available for burn victims. Later in the evening, I heard one of the rescue workers say "It's another Oklahoma City." He was referring to the fact that at this point, few survivors were expected. Later, we would find out that there were not many live casualties beyond the initial wave we had already encountered. So my assignment changed. Captain Feerick asked me to find out how many body bags were in the immediate area and to have them brought to the triage area. That was an unpleasant task to complete.

TIME FOR GRIEF

I heard a loud cheer and clapping coming from the Pentagon. "Finally, survivors!" I thought. I looked over to see a firefighter in one of the windows holding up an American flag. When he brought that flag out, all military personnel stood at attention and saluted. They performed an official flag-folding ceremony. The folded flag was handed to an Army general with three stars. It seemed almost instinctive as several chaplains surrounded the general and started to pray. More and more people joined the circle. It was the first time for many there that they let a tear roll down their cheeks.

I chatted with some of the firefighters during the course of the day and one of them explained to me how they went about fighting a fire from the roof. Earlier in the day my husband, Rick, called and told me that the Twin Towers had collapsed and that over 200 firefighters were killed. "Wow, I can't believe it," I said. "You have no idea, Janet," he said. He wanted me to come home, but I couldn't do that. So as the firefighter was explaining all the details of firefighting and "rehab" that firefighters go through, I mentioned to him what Rick had told me—that the Trade Towers collapsed and about 200 firefighters were missing. "Don't tell these guys," the firefighter said. "They can't know that. They need to be focused."

I didn't say a word to anyone. When I got home, I didn't want to watch the news. I was really happy to see my husband, who was very shook up. I was tired and thirsty. I fell asleep quickly. I dreamt about puppies—white and black faces with big black noses. And I also dreamt that I kept bumping my head on something and saying "Oh shit," and I worried that someone was going to scold me for saying "shit." A sound sleep and two goofy dreams at the end of a day like that. I don't know why. When you ask me how it was that I remained calm and focused during such a horrendous day, all I can say is that I think it was God's hand in my life.

Getting Out of Tower One on 9/11

by Gerry Gaeta

When terrorists connected with the militant Muslim organization known as al Qaeda guided two hijacked airplanes into the two towers of New York City's World Trade Center complex, the devastation was immense. The explosions which followed the impacts killed hundreds outright and left those on the upper floors of the towers trapped by fire. Those World Trade Center employees and visitors on the floors below the impact points were forced to evacuate the buildings as best they could. Thousands of people had to descend the towers' stairwells since the elevators had been shut down in response to the emergency. Many who had the arduous task of climbing down seventy or eighty stories never reached the bottom before the towers, gutted by fire from above, collapsed in succession.

Gerry Gaeta was one of the lucky survivors who did escape Tower One. Gaeta was employed as an architect by the New York and New Jersey Port Authority, the organization charged with the task of managing the Trade Center site. Their offices were located on the eighty-eighth floor of Tower One. Prior to the attacks on September 11, the Port Authority was in the process of redistributing its control over the lease of the site to a company called Silverstein Properties; thus, many Port Authority employees, including Gaeta, were awaiting new positions elsewhere in the organization.

Gaeta was in his office when the first plane, American Airlines Flight 11, struck at 8:45 A.M. EST. Among his other coworkers on that floor was his friend Frank DeMartini, a construction manager for the Port Authority, who did not make it out of the tower. In the narrative that follows, Gaeta describes his tedious escape from the building and his experiences with people he encountered along the way. His description portrays the chaos and fear that were common to many people's reports of the event. Gaeta's narrative concludes with a heartfelt eulogy to those who were lost in the tragedy that day and to the towers themselves.

Gerry Gaeta, "Of Lost Friends, Family, and Buildings," *September 11: An Oral History*, edited by Dean E. Murphy. New York: Doubleday, 2002. Copyright © 2002 by Dean E. Murphy. All rights reserved. Reproduced by permission of Doubleday, a division of Random House, Inc.

Because of the transition to Silverstein, a lot of my staff was applying for new jobs throughout the Port Authority. When I got to work, I had an e-mail waiting for me from a manager at LaGuardia Airport who wanted to talk to me about one of my employees. She was interested in offering him a job. I called her around 8:30 and provided her with the information that eventually helped her to offer him the position. I had just hung up when I heard and felt something ripping through the building. BOOM! BOOM! BOOM! There was a big vibration and the whole tower started to move. The sway was large enough that I could see the ground from my office window on the southeast corner of the floor. The whole building was making a groaning and creaking sound. The steel sounded like it was moaning. I thought we were all going to die, that the building was going to collapse right then and there. It sounded to me like the steel connections were failing, but what was really happening was the building was transferring its load to the steel not taken out by the airplane. But at that moment, I didn't even know about an airplane. My first reaction was that it was an earthquake. Then I thought of a bomb.

LET'S GET OUT OF HERE

I jumped over my desk and ran out the door of my office. My staff was standing there, looking at me, stunned. "That's a bomb," I said. "Let's get out of here." The ceiling had come down in various locations as well as some light fixtures. Smoke and fires were filling the floor. There were three stairwells, one on the east side of the building, one on the south side and one on the west side. We first went to the east stairwell—stairwell B. But when I got to the double doors by the east leg of the corridor, there wasn't anything on the other side. It was extremely dark with black smoke and there was a big hole in the floor. It was just gone where the stairwell used to be. I then headed for the south stairwell, several of my staff following me. We got to the south leg of the corridor, looked out the pair of doors there, and saw that the gypsum board walls around the freight elevator were completely blown down against the stairwell and against the door to the stairwell. They were all piled up and on fire.

We gave up on that exit, and moved toward the north side, where our real estate department was. I went to a window on the north façade and looked outside. All I saw was debris coming down that was on fire. Then I heard the sound of emergency vehicles down below on the street. When I looked around me, the real estate department offices were severely damaged with the office furniture toppled. It was a real mess. The windows along the whole northeast corner were blown out. Something said to me, "You have to get out of here." I must have repeated it aloud, because one of my supervisors later told me that she heard me say it.

Frank DeMartini and others were also working the floor searching for a way out. People were coming up to me, since I was a manager, looking for direction. "What do we do, Gerry?" I said I didn't know yet, but we had to get off the floor. I suggested that we get everyone together and gather our thoughts, so we went into an office on the southwest corner that was large enough and free of smoke. It belonged to our director, Alan Reiss, who was not there that morning.

SOME STAY BEHIND

About that time, Elaine Duch, who worked in the real estate department, was walking down the corridor, her arms stretched out and a purse in her hand. "Help me," she pleaded. Her hair was scorched and her dress was melted to her skin. She looked like she had been badly sunburned all over her body. Her glasses were falling off her face. Anita Serpe saw her and sat her down in Alan's office. Most everyone was there now, about 20 or 25 people. We took correspondence off Alan's desk and tried to block up the cracks between the door and the frame. But it wasn't working. There was still smoke coming in.

I opened the door, and there came Frank. He had gone back to his own office and called a relative to say he was okay and was trying to find a way out. He had been having breakfast on our floor with his wife, Nicole, who also worked in the Trade Center, when the plane hit. I said to him, "Frank, we can't stay here. The smoke is getting bad. I can't breathe. We have people with asthma and a woman who is burned." He looked me in the eye and said, "Gerry, I think stairwell C is open." I said to him, "Okay, Frank, I'm going to take some tissues, and I am going to run for it and see if we can go down that stair. It doesn't make sense to stay here."

Previously there had been a discussion in the office about who wanted to leave. Some people wanted to stay on the floor and wait for help or offer help to others. In Frank's case, he knew there was danger with a fire like that. That's why he sent his wife downstairs with everyone else. She pleaded with him to come too. He told her that he would follow soon. And I believe he did start down after all the other people were off the floor. From talking to colleagues later, I believe that Frank got down at least as far as the 76th floor because he called one of our construction inspectors from there on his radio. He wanted the inspector to send up two structural engineers to evaluate some damage on that floor. No one went up because the police would not allow anyone into the building. Being the person he was and having the knowledge he possessed of the structural design of the building, Frank probably was unconcerned about taking his time coming down, looking at the damage and seeing who else might need help. He knew how the building was constructed. He had only come to the Port Authority a year or so earlier from Leslie Robertson, the structural engineers for the World Trade Center. It wasn't that long ago when he had given an interview to the History Channel. He said the towers "probably could sustain multiple impacts of jetliners." In my opinion, Frank, God rest his soul, never thought the buildings would collapse. But then who did?

DESCENDING THE STAIRS

We finally decided to leave the floor and we ran through the reception area toward the elevator lobby. Frank stood by. He was comforting people, saying, "It's going to be okay, it's going to be okay." I led the way, making a right turn into the corridor adjacent to stairwell C. As I went through the passenger elevator lobby, I saw that there were no walls. They had fallen into the corridor. The hung ceiling was completely collapsed into the floor and there was no lighting. There were live downed electrical wires all around. To be honest, I didn't know if there was even a floor there. I gingerly walked across the fallen debris toward the stairwell door.

I looked down the corridor toward stairwell B, and I saw again that there was only blackness. When I made it to stairwell C and opened the door, to my amazement the battery-powered backup lights were on. I looked inside. The four walls were intact. The stairs were still there. I went down one flight to see what it was like. It looked safe and the smoke had lessened. "Let's go for it!" I yelled up to everyone else.

Elaine was one of the first to come down. She was with Doreen Smith, another secretary who worked in the real estate department. One of the girls who worked for Silverstein had wrapped a sweater around Elaine's waist to give her some decency. There was a big knot in the back tied with the arms of the sweater. Doreen went ahead of Elaine, clearing the way and ready to catch her if she should fall, and I walked behind her, holding on to the knot so she would not fall. We walked 88 floors that way. When we got down to the 76th floor, the stairs led to a crossover corridor that was designed to create a smoke barrier. It was about 50 feet long and had a fire-rated door at each end to provide a smoke-proof enclosure. We went through the first door, but the second door wouldn't open. I kicked it a dozen times but it wouldn't budge. I started to think that maybe this was part of the terrorist plot—that they had calculated in their minds that people would be trying to escape, so they had locked the stairwell doors. In reality, I figured out later, the jolt of the plane hitting the building probably racked and jammed the door. I would also guess that when Frank made that radio call from the 76th floor, he was at the same jammed door and wanted the structural engineers to determine what was wrong.

Thank God I was familiar with the building design, so when we couldn't get through that door, I told everyone we had to turn around and go back to 78, which was the sky lobby floor. When we got there, it was dark but there were four people standing at the end of the lobby. I guess they were Port Authority emergency personnel. "Is there any other stairwell available?" I asked. They said stairwell B was open. We ran across the sky lobby, and I believe we took an escalator down to the 77th floor to get to stairwell B. We had to cross a corridor with water in it and there were electrical wires lying all over the floor. It looked very dangerous, but we had no choice but to continue. "We are going to die waiting here, or we are going to die getting electrocuted," I said to one of my colleagues. We all made it through, thank God. Nearby there were some people trying to save someone who had become trapped in an elevator.

It wasn't until we hit the 50s that we really ran into many people in the stairwell. Knowing Elaine's condition, I started yelling, "Please move to the right! Burn victim!" People moved, but as we passed, many of them got upset when they saw Elaine. Some gasped, "Oh, my God!" while others just started crying. Elaine didn't say a word all the way down. I didn't want her to stop, so I kept saying to her, "Only another ten floors, Elaine. Only another ten minutes." In the low 40s, there was a heavyset black woman being helped by two other people and there were some firemen too. One of the firemen took his extinguisher, opened the top and

poured water over Elaine, Doreen and me to cool us off. We probably looked overheated. Others were stopping and going on the
way down, but with our path cleared the whole way, we were just
going and going.

MAKING IT OUT OF THE TOWER

When we finally got down to the concourse level, I realized how bad
things were. Water was coming down like a waterfall from the ceiling, and it was about 6 inches deep on the floor. The marble on the
walls was cracked. There was a huge gap between the walls and the
ceiling in the core area. And here I was with Elaine, yelling, "Burn
victim! Where do we take her?" We were told to keep walking, that
the EMS and paramedics were through the concourse shopping
mall toward Building 4. When we got about 100 feet into the concourse by The Limited, two paramedics saw Elaine. Each of them
grabbed an arm. They told Doreen and me that they needed to run
to get her to the ambulance. My legs were killing me and I knew I
couldn't run. "I'll go," Doreen said. I told her I would catch up with
them, but they were gone by the time I got to Building 4.

I got out of the concourse by going up the escalator by Building
5. Once outside, I ran into someone from the Port Authority's Port
Commerce Department, Lyngard Knuston. . . . I said to Lyngard,
"Let's go." She started breaking down, and like a scene from Sodom
and Gomorrah, she stared back at the towers, both of them on fire.
"Look what they've done to our buildings!" she cried. I looked too,
and that was the first time I saw that the South Tower had also been
hit. "We have to keep going," I told her.

We walked more but my legs were in such pain that we stopped
for a few minutes and sat on the wall outside Trinity Church. As we
continued past City Hall, we ran into a couple of other people, Bob
and Atef, who also worked for the Port Commerce Department. The
four of us walked north up Broadway. It was eerie because everybody was walking in the same direction with us, but nobody was
saying much. . . .

At about one o'clock we made our way to a pub on 14th Street
to get something to eat. On our way there, some people had told us
that the towers had collapsed, but we kept saying, "You're crazy."
We just didn't believe it. But there was a big-screen TV in the pub
and for the first time the four of us saw the towers fall. I couldn't eat
anything. My heart went to my throat. I had to drink a couple glasses

of water. I started to get upset and sick about the whole thing. I thought about my staff. I realized I had gotten out early, ahead of them, because of Elaine. I started to think about everybody I knew who worked in the complex. The nightmares in my mind started to roll. I still don't believe the towers are gone.

THE JOURNEY HOME

We heard there were ferries running to New Jersey. We decided to go home, so a couple of us who live in New Jersey walked up to 39th Street by the Javits Center to get a ferry across the Hudson River. The line must have been a mile long, but it was moving. . . .

I finally got on a ferry and made it to Hoboken. Once there, they said anyone that was in the towers should exit the boat first. We began making our way toward the end of the boat when they stopped everyone and began to send the boat back out on the river. They said there was a bomb scare in Hoboken and that we were going to Weehawken instead. But we soon turned around again and went back to Hoboken. The bomb threat was removed. They put us in this long procession line, like a cattle run. It looked and felt like one of those scenes from a concentration camp, with everybody being led single file to the gas chambers. We were all in a row and we had to walk this well-defined path. Security people on either side were making sure we didn't step out of line.

They were taking us to a decontamination area, because of the chemicals and asbestos on our clothes. I thought they were going to strip us down. I was thinking, You mean to tell me they have new clothes for everybody here? Instead there were these firemen standing there with hoses spraying everybody. The water was ice cold. Then you had to go through this tent structure, where they had all different kinds of water spray nozzles. At the end, the Red Cross was there and they gave out towels. You had to fill out a card and wear it around your neck on a string. It had bright primary colors associated with HAZMAT coding. We had to complete the card with our name, address and phone number. I was thinking, Oh my God, what are they going to do with us?

Outside the Hoboken terminal where the buses arrive, they had set up a temporary examining center with doctors. I went to one of them, and he put his stethoscope on my chest. "I don't hear nothing," he said. I said jokingly, "What does that mean, I am dead?" Another doctor came over and his stethoscope was working and he heard something. After that, they took the card from around my neck and released me.

I finally got home around 6:30. I remember it was still light out. My wife was across the street talking to our neighbor. When she saw me, she hurried across and we hugged and kissed. Two of my four boys were there, Chris and Michael, and we hugged too. My fourth son, Gerry Jr., was away at college in Newark and witnessed the entire scene at the World Trade Center from his dorm room. My other son, Joseph, was still on his way home from the city. I got cleaned up, put on some sweats and got something to eat. I said I wanted to go to the hospital to get checked out. At the hospital they determined I had some smoke inhalation. They put me on oxygen and they examined my legs. The pain was so bad I couldn't walk for a week without crutches. I had never walked so long and so far before and I am not in the greatest shape. . . .

A BRIEF EULOGY

The loss of the World Trade Center was more than a loss of some buildings. This complex was the pride and joy of the Port Authority and especially of the members of the World Trade Department. When we lost this complex, it was like losing a child. To all of the courageous Port Authority coworkers and friends I lost on that horrible day, may God keep you in the palm of his hands forever and may he be a continuing comfort to all of your families. I miss you all and the complex that made us a family.

Desperate but Thwarted Rescue Efforts on 9/11

by Bertram Springstead, interviewed by Jon Malkin

After the first of two hijacked planes hit the World Trade Center on September 11, 2001, police, firefighters, and Emergency Medical Services (EMS) personnel responded to the scene immediately. The rescue teams set up command posts in the lobbies of the two towers and sent squads of men up the stairways of the 110-story complex in search of survivors and to assess the blaze that was burning eighty stories above.

In the following interview conducted with Battalion Chief Jon Malkin on December 4, 2001, Bertram Springstead, a firefighter in New York's Ladder Company 9, relates his actions on that Tuesday morning. Springstead tells of how he made his way to the firehouse and then rushed to the scene with others who had responded to the call. Arriving at the base of the World Trade Center, Springstead describes the slow plod up the stairwells of Tower One. Weighed down by heavy coats and equipment, many of the rescue workers became exhausted after making it only a quarter of the way up the towers. Springstead and his colleagues reached the twentieth floor before they had to turn back; some of them were too tired to continue, and the lower floors by that time were deserted. Back in the lobby, the rescue teams were given the order to evacuate the building, not realizing the neighboring tower, Tower Two, had just collapsed, killing all the rescue personnel within. Springstead and a few of his team members pushed out into the streets and fought their way through the dense dust cloud that arose from the collapse of Tower Two. As Ladder Company 9 began to regroup, Springstead realized that not everyone in his squad had made it out of the building.

September 11, I remember walking into the kitchen about 8:30 in the morning, sat down, coffee, paper. A little while later, I guess it was about a quarter to 9, somebody came in and said they saw the

Jon Malkin, "Fatal Confusion: The Emergency Response, 9/11 Firefighters: Oral Histories," www.nytimes.com, July 5, 2002. Copyright © 2002 by The New York Times Company. Reproduced by permission.

plane coming over quarters and then they said they saw it hit the trade center.

So we all ran to the corner of Lafayette and Great Jones, and we could see the big hole in the building where the plane had hit. So we all went back to quarters, started getting dressed. We didn't get the call right away. Thirty-two went on the first ticket. We were all sitting in the house watching, bunkering up. Then it came on the TV, and we started watching it on TV, wondering why we didn't get the call yet and complaining that we didn't get the call.

Q. Sure.

A. It was about 5 to 9, I guess, or a couple minutes before 9, I guess, I remember saying to the guys, "I wonder if they're holding this ticket until after 9." Sure enough, the ticket came in 090014.

Q. Get out of here.

A. And I made a copy of the ticket, and I stuffed it in my pocket, because I was like, ". . . I'm calling the union when I get back." We were watching people jump on TV from the building. I said how can they be holding this ticket. That was what was going through my mind the first time.

We get on the rig. We're going down. The probie [probational firefighter], John Tierney, he was off duty before we got out. Something wasn't right that day. I knew something was wrong, and I turned to him and said, "John, do me a favor, don't take this run in. Just stay here. You're off duty, you're not getting paid, just go home, man, just go home." But who is not going to jump on the rig? So he jumped on the rig and he was sitting on a lap.

We were driving down, sirens the whole way down. We get there. We stepped off the rig, and I look up and I noticed that both towers were on fire now. We didn't realize at the time that another plane had hit. We didn't see it and couldn't hear it while responding. I just figured the other tower was on fire from stuff flying from the other building. So we really didn't know there was a second plane.

We parked on I guess it was the northeast corner of the trade center, which is right at Vesey and Church, I guess. Vesey and Church, Vesey and Church right there. We stepped off the rig, and there were plane engine parts and people yelling and screaming. We stepped off and noticed the two towers on fire.

We started walking down Vesey towards West Street. Our assignment was tower one, so we would go into the lobby. Just as we turned onto West Street, we were coming towards the entrance of the trade center and we saw a jumper coming down. We were like,

"Oh, man, look at this." They were smoldering, on fire, smoking. So we were like, "Oh, man." Just a tremendous thump. The noise was unbelievable.

Now we're looking up as we're going in, and we go into the lobby and there's everybody. [Fire Commissioner Thomas] Von Essen's there. The mayor's there. Everybody's at this command post, everyone in white hats. We were standing there at the command post, waiting for our assignment.

The probie still didn't have a mask. He had jumped on the rig, so he was on somebody's lap on the way down there. So I walked over to the command post and took one of the aide's masks and gave it to him and said, "Put this on because we were going up now." [Fire Chief Peter] Ganci took us over to the stairs and said, "Call us when you get there." That's all they said.

Q. Ganci [who died in the building's collapse] was with you in the lobby?

A. He showed us to the stairs. Ganci showed us to the stairs to take. We started walking up. I was taking my time, pacing myself, going nice and slow, taking it easy. Those guys were a little quicker than I was, and they kind of advanced a couple floors beyond me.

SLOW CLIMB

They were up a couple floors ahead of me—I don't know how many—and Don Casey waited for me I guess it was on like the 13th floor—I forget exactly what floor it was on—so that I wouldn't be alone. I was taking my time going up there. We were taking breaks here and there. I forget what floors we took breaks on.

There were a lot of maydays with chest pains on the radios and stuff like that. I don't remember who or what floor, but there were a lot of maydays. E.M.S. was going all over the place with maydays with chest pains.

We got up, and then me and Don were kind of pacing ourselves. We pretty much tried to take a break on every floor that you had access to, because you didn't have access on every floor. So whatever floor you had access, we would go in, take a quick breather and then get going again. I guess it was about the 19th or 20th floor when I said, "Don, I've got to take a break."

I was really hot. I said, "Don, I've got to take this coat off for a second, take a breather." They had water, and people had broken open a Poland Spring machine and there were bottles of water, so we would take a break. I took my stuff off, and I was pouring water all over.

Five Engine was there on the floor, too. Derek Brogan from 5 Engine, he was miserable, miserable: chest pains, nauseous, on his knees. He looked terrible. So we were pouring the water over him. Real bad.

Then Don Casey, who I was with, starts saying his arm was tingling, he's getting numbness in his arm, in his left arm. I was like, "All right, sit down." E.M.S. was there. Two guys from E.M.S. were there. One was working on Derek, and the other guy started working on Casey with the oxygen and stuff like that.

I remember somebody said, "You think you're having a bad day? Take a look out this window." We looked out the Trade Center window, and there was the Vista Hotel, I guess it was there. I'm not really sure what building I was looking at, but I'm pretty sure it was the roof of the Vista. There had to be 30, 40 jumpers sprayed out all over the roof. I went, "Oh, Jesus, what the hell is going on here?"

As I was looking out the window, which is a total of five seconds, another jumper comes by, kind of like clipped the edge of the roof and just vaporized. The guy just disappeared. There was no longer a body, just a big cloud of red.

Q. Wow.

A. I was like, "I didn't need to see that." A total of five seconds I was looking out that window, total.

TOWER TWO COLLAPSES

So I go back, and I was with Don and I was saying, "Maybe we should take you down, Don. Maybe we should start working down if you're getting—" He said, "No, I'm all right now. I'm all right."

The E.M.S. guy was yelling at him. He said, "You guys, I've probably seen this a thousand times. You might be having a heart attack." But Don didn't think so. He thought his suspender strap was too tight, which turned out it was, because he was fine.

There was a time we were like, "Well, I don't know, Case, maybe we should take you down. Let's get out of here. How much farther? Are you going to make it?"

Then 5 Engine was there, the whole 5 Engine was there. Derek Brogan was miserable. He was terrible. He looked terrible. I was nervous about him. He looked really bad. So I turned to 5 Engine officer. They didn't want to leave him, but they wanted to keep going.

I said, "Look, Lou, you want me to take down Derek?" I said, "I'm going to take Don down. Do you want me to take Derek down? I'm taking two," because 5 Engine didn't want to leave another guy behind. He said, "Yeah, maybe that's a good idea, if you're going down." I had a radio, Don had a radio, and this way they didn't have to lose another guy with a radio when it went up.

So maybe, I don't know, five seconds later, that's when tower two must have started coming down. The building started shaking, a tremendous rumbling. Light bulbs were falling out. File cabinets were tipping over.

We were in that corner of tower one that's kind of close to tower two where they kind of like point at each other there. That's the corner we were in. I don't know what the hell was going on, but whatever it was, it was right outside the window that we were standing like five feet from.

Some guys were diving on the floor. Some guys were—I just took off for the other side. I said whatever was going on was on that side. I said I'm getting to the other side of the building. I started running.

We got to that side of the building. I didn't see Casey, but he told me he dove on the floor first. Then when he saw me run by, he said: "That looks like a good idea. Maybe I'll go with Bert and get to the other side." Casey got him to the stairwell. He said, "Let's get the hell out of here." I said, "Hold on, hold on, Case. I don't even know what that was. Let's regroup here. First we've got to go back and get our stuff."

We had taken our coats off. We don't have any tools. We don't have our masks. I said, "Let's go back, get our stuff." I said: "First of all, Brogan is still back there. We're responsible for him now." I said, "Let's go see if we can find Derek."

We get back there. It was dark. Most of the light bulbs had fallen off, so you really couldn't see much. I guess it was from the dust cloud outside there was no light coming in. We didn't know at the time. We just thought it was another plane or something, another explosion or whatever. We really didn't know what it was.

We got our masks and our coats, grabbed the halogen and started looking for Derek, couldn't find him, searched all over. He didn't have a radio. We couldn't call him. Then we got the word on the radio to get out of the building. I was like: "Case, I guess he's gone. There's nobody on this floor." We searched the whole floor. There's nobody there.

THE DESCENT

So we started going down. We made our way to the stair. Then it was just a slow walk down, as slow a 20 floors as you can walk. You took a step, you took another step, took a step. You got to each landing, you opened the door:

"Anybody else here? Let's go. Everybody out." You let a couple people in front of you, another step. . . .

So then we started walking out. It didn't matter. You weren't going anywhere. It was slow walking. We got to about the fifth or sixth floor. It was getting a little smoky, dusty, whatever. Don started to put his mask on. I said, "Don, why don't you save it?" It wasn't that bad yet. I said, "Why don't we get down and see if we need it to get out of here before we waste it up here." So we just started covering up, and we made it all the way down.

We came to the lobby, and the lobby was a disaster. It never registered that the other building had collapsed. We came outside, and we walked the same way we came in. We went back to the—you didn't go through the doors. All the glass was broken on the ground floor when we came in the first time, I guess from the elevators collapsing or I don't know. All the glass was gone.

So we were walking through the plate glass along the wall. We slowly walked our way out towards the sidewalk, making sure that no jumpers were landing on us. I don't know what it was exactly, but I wound up seeing Lieutenant Smith. We just happened to bump into him.

I radioed to him on the way down that me and Case were in staircase B, I think it was, and we were on our way down. He said: "O.K. See you out front." I said, "Do we have everybody?" I forget what he said. I don't know. Everybody was with me on the stairs. I don't see everybody.

OUT IN THE STREETS

But there were people—there were guys all over the place. There were firemen everywhere, wandering around. So we started looking around to see if we could see the guys. I said: "Lou, they've got to be right here. So I'm going to go back inside and maybe they're in the lobby." He said all right, he's going to gather everybody up out here when I find our three guys. I said: "We'll get together up the street. We'll regroup and where are we going.". . .

So I started my way back in underneath that foot bridge right on the corner of Vesey and Church, the same way we walked in. There were a couple rigs there. There was a guy with a bullhorn, a chief. I thought he was a chief. He had a white shirt on. I don't remember if he had a helmet on. But he had a bullhorn, a guy with a bullhorn.

He was yelling: "Clear the area. Clear the area." I really wasn't listening to him. I was kind of walking by. He stopped me. He grabbed me. He said, "You've got to get out of here." I said, "Chief, I'm missing three guys." He said: "Everybody coming out I'm sending this way. They're probably out already. Go up this way. Everybody is going up this way." I said, "Look, Chief, they might be right here." He said, "Get the—out of here now." He had me by my shoulder and he kind of shoved me away.

All right. So now I'm doing the same thing. I'm looking around. There's firemen all over the place now. I'm looking at each guy and I'm going over to guys. It's not really registering. The street is a disaster. There's stuff all over the street.

I was just by the other side of that foot bridge, I guess. You heard somebody, turned around and looked up, and I saw a big section of the facade coming down, straight down. I said, ". . . and I took off up West Street, north on West Street, just ran as far as I could, which wasn't too far before the dust cloud took you out and stuff was hitting you and banging off your mask and your helmet."

SEARCHING THROUGH THE DUST

Then the dust cloud started coming, and I turned around and the cloud was coming and I turned my mask on and put it on. Then it was just dust and dark for it seemed like forever, darker than any fire I had ever been in. There was nowhere to go. You could see it swirling around you. I actually had to push the face piece onto my face to keep it out. It was forcing its way inside.

Then it was just wandering in the dark north on West Street, bumping into cars and barricades and whatever else I bumped into. I finally started coming out of the dust and finally started seeing a little light. I turned around, and now I'm missing all seven guys, the other seven guys that were with me. Now I don't know where anybody is.

So I started looking for guys again. . . .

Q. Where did you last see those guys [three missing men]?

A. I saw them in the lobby going up in the stairs, probably the third floor going up. They were taking off. They were in much better shape than I was. They were flying up the stairs. I'm like I'm pacing myself. We've got 90 floors. I said I'm not going—I'd be dead by the 20th floor if I ran up 20 floors. It was a nice easy pace.

I never saw those guys for the rest of the day. I was with Casey. I bumped into Smith and Warnock. When I saw those guys outside, it was right underneath that foot bridge. That's where I saw those guys. Then I turned around and went back in the lobby.

I saw Mike Maguire. I kind of just waved to him that, hey, be careful of the jumpers.

We were out there. He walked out and met up with those guys. Then everybody scattered when it came down. Guys went off in all different directions. Those guys were walking north on West Street when I went back towards the building to go back in to get the other three guys.

That's the last time—I never saw Walz. I never saw Baptiste. I never saw Tierney. I never saw those guys. I figured they had to be in that lobby, though. I don't know, they must have made a wrong turn in the lobby or something or followed the wrong guy. I don't know. I didn't really see them, so I don't know what they did. Just figured they were in that lobby and I was going to go get them.

That was it. I got back to quarters. Answering the phone putting the family off then. That was pretty much it.

Q. Those three guys are lost?

A. Those three guys are lost.

Q. They never came back?

A. No. I thought for most of the night that we'd find them someplace, whether it was in a hospital. They didn't know where anybody was. I just assumed they got out. I just assumed that those three guys got out. I miss them.

Living in Occupied Ramallah

by Islah Jad

The bloody conflict between Israel and the Palestinians has left countless lives destroyed. Israeli Jews and Palestinian Arabs have been at war with one another for over half a century. It is a struggle that has religious and economic dimensions, but it is primarily a fight over who has a rightful claim to the land where the nation of Israel now stands. The Israelis argue that their current homeland was promised to them in biblical times since they are descendants of the Jewish king Abraham, whose kingdom stood where Israel is now located. They also regard their nation as a sanctuary from Western anti-Semitism, which came to a head during the Holocaust. The Palestinians, on the other hand, claim rights to the land based on their centuries-old residence there.

Since Israel's declaration of independence in 1948, the fighting has rarely ceased. Palestinian activists continually agitate the situation by attacking various Israeli public places with suicide bombings, car bombings, and other militant tactics. These terrorist acts have prompted the Israelis to use their army to occupy the Arab section of the Israeli state in order to quell the Palestinian rebellion.

The Israeli army uses various means to subdue riotous behavior among the Palestinian communities it occupies. Checkpoints, curfews, and even the demolition of Palestinian settlements are just some of the tactics used by the Israeli military to control Palestinians. Many critics insist that these efforts are themselves a form of terrorism. In 2002, the Palestinian city of Ramallah was occupied by the Israeli army because the Israelis believed it to be a haven for terrorist activity. Ramallah is just one of several Palestinian cities to undergo such occupation.

Islah Jad, a lecturer of politics and development at the Women's Studies Institute at Birzeit University, is an Arab resident of Ramallah. In the following narrative, Jad explains the

Islah Jad, "Back to Occupation, Back to 'Normal,'" *Live from Palestine: International and Palestinian Direct Action Against the Israeli Occupation*, edited by Nancy Stohlman and Laurieann Aladin. Cambridge, MA: South End Press, 2003. Copyright © 2003 by Nancy Stohlman and Laurieann Aladin. Reproduced by permission of the publisher.

stresses of living under Israeli occupation. She expresses her frustration at the plight of Palestinian students who are forced to either study amidst artillery shells or not make it to school at all. She describes life in Ramallah as "madness" because, in order to live, one must forfeit control over one's mortality. The only solace, according to her, is to strengthen the sense of community shared by all Palestinians who face the same uncertainty and oppression.

June 24, 2002, occupied Ramallah

It's been a while since I've written. I have needed some time to digest our new situation, one dominated by the presence of the Israeli army. Their presence has never been easy to accept, but what is harder to accept is that we are now back to "normal," and, apparently for Palestinians, this means being in the continuous presence of an occupying army.

OCCUPATION IS A NORMAL WAY OF LIFE

Before the return of the army's visible presence, though, Palestinian lives were not exactly proceeding as normal. For example, I used to leave my house to go to work, to my dear Birzeit University, with my three children and husband. Now, you leave, you intend to arrive somewhere, but you never reach your destination since the army always prevents you from going to study, or to work, or to shop, or to pay condolences, or to visit a friend. Palestinians end up doing everything to prepare for a normal working day—but we never get to work. We return home exhausted, tired of witnessing the constant humiliation, seeing our lovely students waiting in long lines under the searing sun, sometimes beaten, arrested, or shot at, and always cursed at and insulted.

Israeli soldiers the same age as our students have the power to bring an entire academic community of 5,000 people to its knees. Israel dares to call this "fighting terror," but even a child could see that the army's aim is to make the Palestinian people so fed up that they leave their country. What parent could bear to see his or her children wasting their academic years for no good reason? It is excruciating to watch. Maher, my eldest son, still has one month to go before he graduates and cannot finish his studies this month. I think about all the other students and how they are not allowed to go to their universities, not even allowed to be in the streets, lest they become choice targets for the Israeli army. They have no escape: no parks, no theaters, no work, no places to go. How can we make the world see this simple reality and stop talking incessantly about Palestinian "terror"?

LIFE IN RAMALLAH

Yesterday, I was woken at 4 A.M. Helicopters were hovering *so* close to the houses, tanks were roaring below in the streets. By 5 A.M., soldiers announced with loud speakers: "You are forbidden to leave your houses; anyone who does not follow orders will be severely punished or shot!" I realized that there would be no work again today, no school, no newspapers. By 6 A.M., I decided to go back to sleep.

"My son's wedding is supposed to be next week! What am I to do with all the invitation cards, with all the preparations?" said Afaf, my neighbor, who came over to visit me.

"You are not afraid to go out of your house under curfew?" I asked, incredulous at her bravery.

"The tanks just left. They did not come with as many tanks as in the first invasion in March 2002. Instead of 400 tanks and Armored Personnel Carriers, they came with only 70, or so I heard. This means that they know there is no resistance; it is more than enough to come with two tanks. Who can stop them? We have no planes, no missiles, and no rockets. So while the tank goes for a round, I will finish my coffee with you," said Afaf.

We chatted for an hour. We shared our sorrow for all the effort and work of the high school students that goes on in vain. Now they should be taking their final exams. This is the most difficult bottleneck moment in their scholastic lives, after which they apply to universities or go study abroad. And they are being prevented from taking the exams. A whole year is being lost.

Yassmine, my youngest daughter, reminded me of the stress she witnessed last year when she was studying under the tank shells and noise of explosions:

> I was lucky last year; at least I managed to pass my exams. These poor students cannot even *take* theirs. What will they do? What future awaits them? They try to do the right thing, prepare themselves for a good life, and they are stopped. And

if they become suicide bombers, they are called terrorists. Who is terrorizing whom in our situation?

Today, at 6:30 A.M., I awoke to another loudspeaker announcing the lifting of curfew from 7 A.M. to 12 noon. I didn't want to wake up. I did not feel like leaving my house or buying anything, I did not want to see the soldiers or what they did to the city again, but then I remembered my toothache, my daughter's papers that needed to be sent to get a US visa, and many other "plans." I began to organize my thoughts to see what I could do.

Suddenly Saleh, my husband, who went out once he heard the call lifting the curfew, came back running. "Don't go out! They are shooting. They shot a Palestinian in the head and he is dying in the Red Crescent Hospital!" said Saleh.

"But they announced lifting the curfew!" I replied.

"Yes, they did the same thing in Jenin three days ago, but then they fired a tank shell and killed four people, including three children who were playing around, so don't listen to what they say," said Saleh. "They want to *appear* as if they are lifting the curfew, and that we are *choosing* not to leave our houses, so stay where you are until we see where this madness is taking us!" . . .

MAINTAINING SANITY

I began to wonder if we are all going to reach a point where we choose not to leave our homes even when curfew is lifted because we do not want to be injured or killed? When I reached that point, though, I decided that if I want to keep my sanity, it is better not to think about plans, needs, death, life, or anything. When you control nothing in your life, why burden yourself with thinking of how your plans will be aborted, how your life could be lost for buying some food or sending some papers?

I instead decided that I would gather strength from friends and neighbors who witnessed worse situations. Ali, my colleague at Birzeit, lost his house and all his belongings in less than one hour. "They did not allow my children to get their books to prepare for their exams," he told me. "They did not allow us to take anything from our house. Sixteen families became homeless in one hour in the middle of the night!" Ali used to live in the Abu al Kassem, a six-story building built by a Palestinian American who came back from the United States to invest his money. "They surrounded the building at 2 A.M. looking for one single 'wanted' person, but when they did not find him, they evacuated the building and shelled it with tanks from three directions," he said. Ali told me:

> One of the Israeli officers started crying when his wife called him on his cell phone. He did not like what was going on. But then another officer told us, "1 wish you were all inside while I shelled the building!" We did not know where to go or what to do. We are still sleeping in our neighbors' houses. The owner of the building had a heart attack. So did Rawda's husband, who just finished the renovation of his flat. He had spent more than $7,000 to refurbish after the mess caused by the soldiers when they used his home as a base in the first invasion. He had to start from zero again, but now everything is in rubble. His heart could not take it anymore, a man of 40 years lying in bed with a heart attack with no place to go, no money to start again, and, most important, no heart to grieve.

> But you know what I said to this officer who wanted to shell us in our houses: "You start counting from now. My son, who you forbade from taking his books, is now nine years old. In eight years time, I myself, his father, will send him to kill you in your own city and maybe in your own house if he can—remember that!"

It was funny then to hear President Bush talking about how Palestinian independence is hindered by corruption and a lack of political reform, that Palestinians should start by reforming our political system and changing our corrupt leaders. I wanted to tell him "But Mr. President, it is not Arafat[1] who is killing our children, shelling our houses, causing despair to our children to go and kill themselves, or making us homeless in an hour, but rather it is your friend, your 'man of peace,' Ariel Sharon, with his 'moral,' but at least now visible, occupation army." Please, at least give us a break.

---

1. Yasser Arafat, chairman of the Palestine Liberation Organization

Mourning a Victim of a Palestinian Bomber

by Dina Pinner

When Israel declared statehood in 1948, the Palestinian Arabs, then living on land claimed by the Jews, were left without a homeland. This fueled a bitter resentment among the Palestinians. Without an army of their own or even a government structure, some Palestinians turned to terrorist acts to vent their anger and perhaps to force the Israelis to leave the region. Instead, the shootings, car bombings, and other acts of terror prompted the Israelis to use their military to crack down on Palestinian settlements in an effort to root out the terrorists and keep control of the Arab populace. For half a century, the two sides have continued to retaliate against each other's violent behavior, leaving thousands of dead and injured.

As the following article indicates, it is primarily the innocent civilians who fall victim to the conflict between Israel and Palestine. In this narrative, Dina Pinner mourns the loss of Gila, a nineteen-year-old victim of a Palestinian bomb. Gila was a family friend and potential bride of Dina's brother Daniel. She was waiting at a Jerusalem trempiada, a roadside shelter where people hope to flag down rides, when an Arab suicide bomber struck and killed seven people, including Gila. Pinner's grief at the loss of one so full of life is stirred by the fact that Gila had done nothing to deserve her fate. She decries the heartlessness of Palestinians who, she says, insist on agitating the Jewish community and mercilessly taking Jewish lives. Pinner fails to see how Arabs could let this violence go on when they too suffer needless grief. Easing her sadness is her attempt to keep Gila alive in memory.

I will always know what I was doing at 7:30 P.M. on Wednesday [19 June 2002] because that's the day the world became smaller and will never be completely full again. Everyone in Israel has their own

Dina Pinner, "Wednesday Night on French Hill," www.wzo.org.il, July 15, 2002. Copyright © 2002 by the World Zionist Organization. Reproduced by permission.

date. This is mine. This essay is about life without Gila Kessler who was killed the third Wednesday of June 2002, on French Hill. She was my brother's best friend.

EVERYONE KNOWS A VICTIM

Everyone here in Jerusalem, this ever beautiful city, knows someone now who has been killed, if not directly, then someone who knows someone. I am now that someone and it is a tragedy, I wish I wasn't. . . .

Here, summer has kicked in and we can no longer rush. Our pace has slowed, is deliberate, every extra effort considered as the sun beats down. Still at night we wear sweatshirts. As hot as the day gets, still the Jerusalem air does not burn forever.

I miss Gila, am still overwhelmed by her absence. I cannot really believe that she's dead. I saw her grave, was at her *levaya* (funeral) and *shiva* [a period of mourning following the burial] and still I cannot believe it. I saw the pictures on the news and still I ask, how can it be Gila?

And, of course, I wonder for what, ask inane questions like, will the Palestinians have a better state because she is dead? Will [Palestinian Liberation Authority chief Yasser] Arafat use the millions he has laundered to build decent sanitation in Gaza now that Gila has been murdered? And then I hear Gila smile at me ruefully, "what clever questions you ask," she is saying sarcastically, "dwell on that instead, that will help your grieving."

The day before, on the 32A, near Tzomet Pat, Gila's former neighbour was killed. In Eli, Gilo and Ofra they go *shiva* crawling, here in West Jerusalem we write about it, in the Galut you read about it.

There is a sadness that exists now that does not lift. It hangs over me today and will not shift for some time. Gila is dead and I miss her. I miss her as a small voice in the corner, you will never see me again, who will take care of Daniel? You must be that younger sister now.

My older brother, Daniel, misses her more, a daily calling of no-one at the end of the phone when it doesn't ring because Gila has been killed. I love you, you are my best friend, who will be my unconditional acceptor now? And I don't know.

Her mother misses her more, more than I can begin to describe, more than those without wombs, who will never create anything but random ideas, will ever fathom. . . .

DO THE PALESTINIANS MOURN?

When someone goes missing in the Palestinian Authority does no-one notice?

Do Palestinians have best friends?

Don't Palestinians miss people who aren't there?

What happened to the screaming grieving Arab women burying their dead children in the 1980's and 90's?

Does sadness not exist when Palestinians die because they murdered Jews?

Gila Kessler is 19, or she was when she was killed. She was doing *Sherut Leumi*, National Service in *Kiriyat Moriah*, the main education building of the Jewish Agency. She works in the communications room—if you have been present at a video link up with Israel, she will have helped to organise it—and had an interview a week earlier to go to Sweden next year to work with the Jewish community there. She is short, has long dark hair and a taste for garish shoes. She is rebellious, contemptuous of rules and irresistibly charming. . . . Only she isn't anymore, but to write in the past is to accept that she has passed, and that cannot be done yet. . . . I wanted her to marry my brother. . . .

The oldest daughter of a Tunisian mother and American father and older sister to three younger siblings, my brother is like an older brother to her. So I love her as I do my younger self with softness and forgiveness, tinged with sadness. I delight in their relationship and am comforted in the knowledge that it can exist and did until it was destroyed. . . .

WHEN FRIENDS DIE

On that Wednesday night Gila was standing at the *trempiada*, the place where you flag down a lift, on French Hill, on the way home from The *Kiriyat*. My brother usually takes her home but tonight he was visiting his ex-girlfriend, whom none of us likes, in hospital.

Watching the very first pictures of the attack, someone who works with her saw a body wearing bright blue platform trainers. And then the phone calls started.

I do not have a recognisance plan for my friends dying.

I have one for what I will do when I am in a bombing, each scenario taken care of, like if I'm in the *shuk*, market, on a Friday I'll just go home and make other Shabbat arrangements, but always buy the chicken when I first arrive—and that's what I do every week and what I did the time I was there when the 5th bomb went off there in 17 months. I missed the first four.

If I were to be in a random *tachana mercazit*, Central Bus Station, I would close my eyes and walk away and take a taxi home—whatever the cost—and make sure at all costs that I see nothing, I know that what I could see is much more frightening than what could happen to me.

But I have no plans for when my friends die.

NO CONSOLATION

My brother stayed in my flat that Wednesday night. . . .

I try to console my brother but he is having none of it. . . .

Like our mother, the Holocaust refugee who grew up in pre–State Israel, my brother protects no-one from his mourning and pain. He tells it over and over again.

"Gila was murdered yesterday," he says it to people on the phone, "Gila, on French Hill, murdered."

And I say, "my brother's best friend was one of the 7 from yesterday" or "my brother was very close to one of the people yesterday, you know, in French Hill, the man who blew himself up." But the truth is that however we say it it is no softer, no less true, no less tragic. The aching is no less gentle when I say it and my brother walks around like a lost person, not sure what he's meant to do. There is something he knows he has forgotten to do and cannot quite put his finger on it and life is never going to be the same again.

Yet there is manageable and unmanageable loss in all this.

My sweet, funny, bolshie friend once removed I can manage and talk about and write about. I have good memories of her, usually protecting my brother from himself because she saw in him a softness that her father never had for her, a softness that I presume exists in my brother because he is my brother that I've never seen—because he is my brother.

My pain is a quiet thud that dwells in the corner of my stomach assuring me that there will be better days because I know nothing. I can only comfort my brother and he can only comfort Gila's mother.

At her funeral she calls to her from the moment the first *Hesped*, talk, begins until the last person leaves her house at the Shiva and then on and on to Gila, until she can finally sleep.

As White European men talk and talk at this Religious Zionist funeral the weeping of Gila's Tunisian mother does not cease. As the men say words that thud and crash around our heads through a microphone, tears fall and cry to the ground flowing softly, constantly, from women who know their pain and do not talk about it.

By the graveside Gila's mother calls to 4 different peoples, in each of their languages. In Arabic she shouts at Arafat and his supporters for killing her baby, her oldest, the first. In French she tells men, I hate you, you hate me, I never want to see your country again [because France once ruled Tunisia]. In English she asks forgiveness from women, I tried the best with my children, they are good kids, I love them. In Hebrew she pleads with God to save her, to show her a little mercy, today, for once.

And while the men *daven Mincha*, pray, we remain by the graveside comforting her, hug her, let her shout and cry, louder, louder, Gila, Gila, Gila.

WE MUST LIVE ON

Today there is a sadness in my world now that is not shifting. I know that one day it will but for today it is here, lingering above my heart that is mourning the loss of a speck of unconditional brightness that was here just days ago.

In the following days when I go to work and pop into Gila's office where I am greeted by the cat that she had adopted. An ugly, scrawny, Jerusalem rodent, Gila had decided to save it. She never named it, took it to the vet, deloused it, but fed and gave it water, stroked it and let it take cover in her office from the midday rain and then heat. After weeks and months of never having a name and being ignored by Gila's colleagues the cat has been named Yo Yo as in "Yo! Whassup?!" that Gila learned to say when she was in America and understands the ridiculousness of a woman in a long skirt saying it and it always makes us laugh.

During those days Gila's picture is up in the hallway of *Kiriyat Moriah* and a candle burns for her for one week. At the end of the week the candle is removed but her picture remains and we continue on.

For now, and then, we who knew her remember her and miss her.

She is dead and we are at war and we must live on, take hold of the joy and beauty wherever it presents itself and love it. When it goes we know that we were happy to have it. I am happy that Gila Kessler touches my life, it is richer because of her.

CHAPTER 3

Remembrance and Retribution

At the Trial of the Kenyan Bombing Suspects

by Mellina Fanouris

In the following article, Mellina Fanouris recounts her experience at the trial of four Muslims accused of detonating bombs that destroyed the U.S. embassies in both Nairobi, Kenya, and Dar es Salaam, Tanzania, on August 7, 1998. According to news reports, these acts were carried out by the terrorist group al Qaeda in protest of U.S. presence in the Middle East. Over five thousand people were seriously injured or killed in the Nairobi explosion. Fanouris's sister Phaedra was among those killed. The U.S. government made it possible for families of bomb victims to travel to New York City in April 2001 to be present at the court hearings of the accused, so Fanouris, her husband, Lukas, and ten family members joined other families in making the trip.

In her narrative, Fanouris relates her anger at the smugness of the four accused men, as well as her surprise in discovering that their counsel is comprised of American attorneys. She finds it hard to accept that Americans could represent foreign criminals who brutally killed other Americans.

Although Fanouris does not mention it, the accused were convicted for their crime. She does, though, state that during a debriefing prior to the family's return to Nairobi, Fanouris and other members of her group came to a common understanding that al Qaeda must be thwarted if America is to remain safe.

T he aftermath of the bombing was catastrophic. People scrambled through mountains of stones and rubble to look for survivors. While the injured were transported to hospitals, Kenyans from all walks of life, regardless of ethnic or religious background, displayed remarkable solidarity in the face of the tragedy. Heartwrenching were the moments when loved ones couldn't be found or identified.

Among those lost was Consul General Julian Bartley who only

minutes before the bomb was detonated, had helped his staff deal with an unusually high volume of visa applicants. Many of those innocent applicants, patiently waiting for a chance to study in the States, perished in the blast.

The hands of terrorists had deprived the victims of the best way to close down a life—experiencing the full circle of life from beginning to end. Ironically, the terrorists hadn't spared the lives of innocent Muslims who were also caught up in their evil web. Among them was Farhat Sheikh, the Embassy's chief cashier, who was a devout Muslim. He left behind his young wife Nasreen, and three children, the eldest, 18-year-old Farin, only a few months away from joining a college in the States.

"Next weekend," he had told Phae, "I am taking my family on safari. It is my young son's birthday." Sadly, none of his plans would ever materialize. Sheikh had been the bread-winner of his family. Now, their future was uncertain, their dreams shattered.

Hundreds of families were facing the same predicament. They buried their loved ones without being given a chance of saying good-bye, or even laying a comforting hand on their heads.

Five thousand people in Kenya alone were seriously injured, blinded and scarred for life. Further casualties were suffered in a parallel explosion in Dar-es-Salaam, the capital of Tanzania, a neighboring state. . . .

THE TRIAL BEGINS

In April 2001, the U.S. Government arranged for victims' families to attend the ongoing trial of those accused of conspiracy and murder and the bombing of the U.S. Embassies in Nairobi and Dar-es-Salaam.

Lukas and I, together with another ten family members, were met at JFK Airport and taken to the luxurious Marriott Hotel at the World Trade Center.

After only a few hours of sleep, feeling jet-lagged and tired, we were escorted to the Department of Justice and the court room of Judge Sands. Members of the prosecution, whom we had previously met in Nairobi during a briefing on the impending trial, were busy organizing their papers for the day's hearing. The victims' families were placed two rows behind the accused. It was a closed hearing and no press were allowed to attend. In a corner on our right, an artist sat quietly preparing her board and crayons for a sketched impression of the proceedings.

The four accused—Mohammed Rashid Daoud Owhali of Saudi Arabia, aged 24; Khalfan Khamis Mohammed, citizen of Tanzania, 27; Mohammed Saddiq Odeh, a Jordanian, 35; and Wahid Hage, a naturalized American, 40, were escorted into the courtroom by U.S. Marshals. Their hands and feet were shackled.

Like characters in a play, we saw them all go through the motions of being unshackled and guided to their seats. They stretched their arms above their heads, two of them took off their Islamic caps and ran their fingers through their hair before putting them back on. They showed no remorse. One of them looked utterly bored. He kept turning around and giving us intimidating looks, while playing with a pencil in his mouth.

These were the men who had deprived Phae of reaping the fruits of her hard-earned labor, of seeing Paulie through university and of holding her grandchildren in her arms. She had been just three years short of retirement. A feeling of tremendous outrage gripped my throat and I could hardly keep my hands from trembling and knees from knocking. . . .

The Judge rapped his gavel quite ferociously, bringing the court to order. Members of the jury entered from a side door and took their seats. Court was in session.

REACTIONS TO THE TRIAL

I was quite shocked when I observed that two American defense lawyers had been designated to each of the accused. They had been appointed by the Federal Government so as to provide the accused with constitutional protection and give them a fair trial. I knew that they had a job to do, and hated to be judgmental. However, I found this very difficult to accept, especially when they persistently impugned the testimony of the eye witnesses.

By the end of our week in New York, we had developed a certain closeness with members of our group. We were able to interrelate and express our grief to one another. At a debriefing, shortly before we were to return to Nairobi, we reached a consensus: Unless al Qaeda's terrorists were stopped, the atrocities could, one day, pierce the heart of America.

Less than five months later, on the morning of 11 September 2001, the world was horrified and shocked by the barbaric strike on the World Trade Center. The cruel events of that devastating day, and the horror days that followed, will be imprinted in people's minds for as long as they live. The pain, torture and grief for all those who perished in that gutless act of terrorism can never be forgotten.

I thought back of the World Trade Center, rising over the narrow streets of lower Manhattan—and the famous Twin Towers, each 110 stories—almost half a kilometer high. At the very top stood Windows on the World, the famous restaurant 107 stories up. But the Center was much more than that. It covered over six hectares, comprised of seven buildings and had the population of a modest-sized city. Some 50,000 people worked there, and another 80,000 visited it on any given day.

The Center was home to the movers and shakers of the financial world. Indeed it had been built largely for those who bartered and bargained in the global market place. From that spot in lower Manhattan deals were made that shaped lives worldwide. The complex served as a nerve center. Over a dozen branches of U.S. city, state, federal as well as foreign governments held office space in the Center.

The basement housed the great core columns of the towers, a shopping center, an underground railway line and a parking garage for 2,000 vehicles. The place was constantly bustling from early morning to late at night when the subway stopped operating.

Terrorists had destroyed the most populated skyscraper in the world.

KENYA VICTIMS' MEMORIAL

America is greatly admired for honoring their dead and handsomely taking care of victims' families who served them with loyalty and sacrificed their lives for their country. The U.S. is known to be the patriarch of human rights—fairness and equality for all.

In Nairobi, where the once immaculate and imposing American Embassy stood, is a beautiful garden with well-tended flowers and lush green grass, trimmed and cared for. Indelibly engraved on granite are the touching words: "May the innocent victims of this tragic event rest in the knowledge that it has strengthened our resolve to work for a world in which man is able to live alongside his brother in peace." The same-sized lettering is used to name the victims with no discrimination as to their nationality—American, Greek, or Kenyan. They are listed side-by-side, just as they lost their lives.

The Execution of Timothy McVeigh

by Members of the Media

After a jury trial in Colorado returned a guilty verdict on June 2, 1997, Timothy McVeigh, the perpetrator of the Oklahoma City bombing, was sentenced to die by lethal injection on May 16, 2001. The execution date, however, was delayed when Attorney General John Ashcroft uncovered evidence that had not been examined during the trial. But even in light of the new evidence, McVeigh declined to appeal his case, and the sentence was eventually carried out on June 11, 2001.

Gathered at the federal prison in Terre Haute, Indiana, were only a select few witnesses to McVeigh's death. Some of those assembled were relatives of the bombing victims as well as supporters of McVeigh; the remaining were news reporters from various media networks. They watched as McVeigh was harnessed on a table and given a series of drugs that eventually ended his life. He said no last words but left the poem "Invictus" (Latin for "Unconquered") as his final statement. This poem, by William Ernest Henley, speaks of stoic perseverance and self-righteous determination in the face of all obstacles.

The following article gathers taped eyewitness reactions from seven of the ten news reporters who watched McVeigh's death from a small observation room that adjoined the execution chamber.

Byron Pitts, CBS News: Good morning. I'm Byron Pitts from CBS News. . . .

Timothy James McVeigh died with his eyes open. When the curtains came back, he made eye contact with his people who came to support him. When the curtain passed the media center, Mr. McVeigh seemed to look up and intentionally make eye contact with each of us. Then when the curtain passed, the room where the victims' relatives were—and survivors—he turned his head to the right and made eye contact with them.

He did not speak. But Mr. McVeigh did make a—write out a written statement that the warden passed out to each of us. I'll read it to you now. It reads—and this is written by Timothy McVeigh by hand: "Final written statement of Timothy McVeigh. Out of the night that covers me, Black is the Pit from pole to pole, I thank whatever gods may be for my unconquerable soul. In the fell clutch of circumstance, I have not winced nor cried aloud. Under the bludgeoning of chance, my head is bloodied but unbowed. Beyond this place of wrath and tears looms but the horror of the shade and yet the menace of the years finds and shall find me unafraid. It matters not how straight the gate, how charged with punishment the scroll. I am the master of my fate. I am the captain of my soul." He signs it at the end, June 11, 2001.

Thank you.

Shepard Smith, FOX News Channel: I'm Shepard Smith from Fox News Channel. We were taken in as a group. . . .

We were standing at a glass window about 18 inches from his feet. He was wearing sneakers, you could see that. There were sheets up to here and folded over. His hands were down. He looked straight at the ceiling. When the curtains opened, to his left were his representatives. He sat up as much as he could in that chair and looked toward his window and nodded his head like that. Then came toward the media window where there were 10 of us, plus five people from the prison, plus two media representatives as well.

He seemed almost to be trying to take charge of the room and understand his circumstances, nodding at each one of us individually, then sort of a cursory glance toward the government section. He lay there very still. He never said a word. His lips were very tight. He nodded his head a few times. He blinked a few times.

Then when we were told that the first drug was administered, his very tight lips and his very wide eyes changed considerably; his lips relaxed, his eyes relaxed, he looked toward the ceiling where there happened to be a camera staring right at Oklahoma City. And at that point his eyes seem to roll back only slightly, his body seemed to relax, his feet shifted just a bit. There was the administration of one drug and then another, and after the last drug, there was a very slight movement here.

It was like standing on the other side of a glass wall and looking directly at a hospital bed. Tim McVeigh right at us, his hair very short, almost yellow.

The only change between the prison jumpsuit shot that we all knew so well and today's Tim was he seems to have aged a little bit, and he chose to say nothing.

Linda Cavanaugh, KFOR-TV reporter: My name is Linda Cavanaugh. . . . I'm with KFOR-TV in Oklahoma City. The last time I saw Tim McVeigh was in the courtroom in Denver. He had changed markedly. He was paler, he was thinner, and he did not have the same look of arrogance that he had in the courtroom in Denver.

Today, when we came in, his head was almost shaven, as they have described. He was laying flat, but as the windows, as though you were in a bed and you were trying to see what was over the edge of it, he strained his neck to look at us. His lips were partly open, his eyes were open and when they started administering the drugs, he began staring at the ceiling.

After the first drug was administered, his lips began turning a little bit paler, his skin became pale. After they administered the next drug, it appeared that he was breathing through his mouth for the first time, as though he was trying to control his breathing. He took two or three breaths like that and then from that point on for the next several minutes, when the final drug was administered until he was pronounced dead, there was no additional movement from Timothy McVeigh.

It was a very orchestrated, clinical procedure.

I think it went fairly much as they had planned it. The marshal who was in the room and the warden who were in the room stood with their arms crossed in front of them, seldom looking at Timothy McVeigh. And the atmosphere in the press room was one of almost wonderment at what was transpiring in front of you: watching a man die.

The procedure began when they said, "We are ready. You may proceed." At that point, they began the execution process. It culminated when the warden pronounced him dead at 7:14.

Susan Carlson, WLS Radio, Chicago: My name is Susan Carlson. I'm a reporter with WLS Radio in Chicago.

When we walked in the room, we saw him just a few feet in front of us, and he was wrapped tightly in a white sheet. And he almost looked like a mummy. And he deliberately lifted up his head and looked at one of us each by each. He took the time to make eye contact with each of us. And he was slowly nodding as he was looking at each of us across the room, the media witnesses, and the relative and the victim witnesses who were in a room adjacent to us.

After he looked at everybody, he put his head back down and he stared straight up at the ceiling. And his eyes did not move from that position for the rest of the procedure. In fact, I didn't even see him blink once after they started administering the drugs. And he died with his eyes open. As he laid back in position and they started administering all the drugs, his breathing became a little more shallow.

At one point, he filled up his cheeks with air and then just kind of let it go. But I don't believe that was his last breath. There was still some shallow breathing that followed. His skin began to turn a very strange shade of yellow towards the end. And he remained extremely rigid.

I think as a reporter, you cover a lot of things and we've seen dead bodies, but the most chilling part of this was the fact—for me at least—that he took the time to look up and look at each of us in the eye and there was almost a sense of pride as he nodded his head, laid back down, and seemed very resigned to his fate.

He didn't have anything to say, but his poem—the written statement that he handed to—that he handed out before—that he wrote before he passed on indicated that same sense of pride, that this was what had to be done, what he did and what happened to him today was all part of his plan, and he seemed very content and very resigned to the fact that he was going to die and he did not fight it and he almost looked proud of what had happened.

Rex Huppke, Associated Press: My name is Rex Huppke. . . . I'm with the Associated Press. Let me give you a better idea of sort of the time line of how things unfolded. The first thing that we heard in the room, through the speakers, which were in the ceiling, was the warden's voice, saying "Testing one, two, three." He was checking the feed to Oklahoma City. That happened at about 7:02.

We heard his voice come back on about a minute later, saying, "Having a little trouble with the video, just like I said, OK?" Now, the curtains were still drawn, so I can't say for sure if he was speaking to McVeigh or not, but it sounded like it. The testing went on, then his voice came on again at about 7:05. Again, he said the same thing, "Testing one, two, three." And then we heard him say, at 7:06, "We're ready."

Then the curtains were pulled. As they've described, McVeigh looked—he looked first towards his lawyers—or towards his witnesses which included his lawyers, and he kind of shook his head towards them.

Then, he looked at the media and kind of bounced his head towards each one of us. And then he looked over to his right towards the victim witness room, which was a tinted glass pane so he couldn't see into it, but he looked over and he sort of—not real dramatic, but he sort of squinted a little bit, like he was trying to see through the tinted glass to see if he could see anything.

At 7:10, they announced that the first drug had been administered. At that point, he was still conscious, it seemed. His eyes were open and blinking a little bit. Very slowly, his eyes stopped moving. And his head was really perfectly lined up; he wasn't to one side or the other, he was very rigid and straight up and down; and the eyes just sort of started to slowly move back just a little bit.

The second drug was administered at 7:11. Then, at that point was where we saw some of the—not really spasms, exactly, but you saw a couple of heavy breaths and then that was, by and large, it. There was a little stomach movement. And at 7:15 they announced that the final drug had been administered—I'm sorry, at 7:13.

Then at 7:14, the warden came on through the speaker again and announced that he had died.

Nolan Clay, *The Daily Oklahoman:* I'm Nolan Clay. . . . I'm with *The Daily Oklahoman*, Oklahoma City. I just have a few more details. The poem was the "Invictus" poem, that British poem that was written in the 1800s. We all had a copy of it off the Internet. I compared it to the written statement that was given to us. I'll see if we can get copies to the people. Can you make copies of this (inaudible)?

OK. At the top, it says final written statement of Timothy McVeigh. His signature is this scribbled thing that sometimes Mr. McVeigh would write, and it has June 11, 2001. We compared it to the poem. It seems to be word-for-word, punctuation and all that.

Let me give you a few more details. The warden at one point said, "Marshal, we are ready. May we proceed?" And then the marshal picked up a red phone and said, "This is the U.S. marshal to the Department of Justice Command Center. May we proceed?" Something was said back to him. And then the marshal, who was Frank Anderson, said, "We may proceed with the execution."

McVeigh was wearing a white T-shirt. The sheet came up to right about here. You could see the shoulders. The I.V. tubes looked to be yellow and gray. They came from a slot in the wall behind us. He did look to be hooked up to an EKG machine. There was a black line. And he did stare straight up, his eyes—dying with his eyes open is correct.

His eyes did roll back slightly. I also saw the gulping breath, where his cheeks bubbled up. And I saw that twice. . . .

Kevin Johnson, *USA Today:* My name is Kevin Johnson with *USA Today.* . . . I'll take you outside the execution chamber a little bit. We were dropped off on, I guess, the main entrance. We walked up a path to a 13-foot-high chainlink fence topped by razor wire with a couple of heavily-armed guards out front. And then we were ushered in.

I thought perhaps the most remarkable part of it was, as other people have suggested here or have said here, reported here, that his eyes, his line of sight followed the roll of the curtain from right to left, passing first the attorney's window—or his witnesses' window, then ours, past the government witnesses, and then past the victim witnesses from Oklahoma City.

As others have stated, he did strain himself from the gurney to look at each window. And as others have reported here, he did make eye contact with each of us, or at least tried to do that.

Once that happened, though, it was relatively unremarkable in the sense that he—of his expression. He moved his head back and never moved it from that position, staring straight at the ceiling. His eyes became increasingly glassy, almost watery as the process went on. However, before the first drug was administered, I think we all saw these couple of deep breaths, quick swallows, and then a fluttered breath from his lips. And then not much movement after that, perhaps a slight chest movement, as others have reported here before.

Toward the end of the process, sometime before the warden pronounced time of death, it wasn't clear—or at least any signs of breathing were not visible to us. And he appeared, again, as others have reported, to—his eyes were completely glassy at that point. And his skin color turned from almost a very, very pale when we first saw him to a light, light yellow. His lips also turned that color as well.

Visiting Ground Zero

by Robert Klein Engler

When the World Trade Center collapsed on September 11, 2001, it destroyed a dozen other structures around it. The resulting pile of rubble filled the surrounding city blocks, and the dust from the collapse settled all over lower Manhattan. Rescue workers combed the wreckage for several days, but no survivors were found. Then, the 1.8 million tons of debris were excavated and taken away load by load. The site—known as Ground Zero—was not entirely cleared until May 30, 2002.

Since then, hundreds of thousands of visitors have come to view the gaping hole in the earth where the Twin Towers once stood. A fence surrounds the area, and visitors can read the history of the World Trade Center and view famous images from signboards that are tacked along the barrier. A permanent memorial will eventually be erected on the site.

Robert Klein Engler, a professor at Roosevelt University in Chicago, is one of many visitors to New York who felt compelled to pilgrimage to Ground Zero. Engler has written many articles for periodical and news publications, including the following Ground Zero narrative for *American Daily*. In it, he describes his encounters with other visitors as well as his own reaction to viewing the great "absence." Among his emotional responses is a nagging fear that, as the country moves on, the tragedy of September 11 may be forgotten or possibly even ignored.

NEW YORK CITY—The clerk at the Chelsea Savoy Hotel says I could take the subway to Ground Zero. "By the way," she adds, "get a round trip ticket. The Rector Street stop does not sell Metro-Cards for the ride back."

It is a nice afternoon, so I will take the train from 23rd and Seventh Ave. The number 1 or 9 will get me to Rector Street, and then it is just a short walk. Although I've been to New York City before, my business never took me inside the World Trade Center. Now, I am going to view its emptiness. As I turn to leave the registration desk, I see a sign on the hotel wall: "If You Suspect Terrorism Call the NYPD."

Yesterday, on my way to New York City, I was on the train out of Chicago with a man and his young son from Los Angeles. He told me at dinner that he is taking his son to see the Yankees. When I ask him if he is going to visit Ground Zero, he replies almost automatically, "You got to!" I remember also, the words of a woman from the city. When I asked her how she felt that September day, 2001, she answered, "I felt violated." I think about her comment now as I turn the corner on Seventh Avenue. That word "violated" holds such significance for women. Maybe a country can feel being raped, too.

The 1 train going downtown is hardly busy for this time of day. I look at the faces of the people around me and try to imagine their lives. Then I notice a placard in the car that reads: "If You See Something, Say Something—Be Suspicious of Anything Unattended." In a few stops I am at the Rector Street Station. I see nothing unattended. It is then up the stairs, past the turnstiles and out into the warm, July evening. A short walk up Greenwich Street leads directly to Ground Zero.

A PROFOUND ABSENCE

Once there, I stand amazed. The city has put up a galvanized fence to keep the tourists back. Still, many come just as I do, regardless of the fence, to get as close as they can and to stare across and down the hole. It's only five in the evening, but I can hear Spanish, Chinese, and French spoken by the visitors here. There are even languages spoken that I do not recognize.

I am in New York City on business, but feel compelled to come here first. I made up my mind to do it even before I left home. I suppose I did it the way others make up their mind to go on a pilgrimage. Now, I realize Americans ought to make a trip to Ground Zero if they can, in order to see for themselves what hatred has wrought. They should do it before the new building goes up just to sense the magnitude of the hole where the World Trade Center used to stand. Television does not convey the extent of the destruction. On TV things are only as big as the screen. Looking across the empty blocks, that image on TV shrinks to the size of a postage stamp, when in fact the reality of absence is an expanse of 16 acres and profound.

I suppose if you took the Great Pyramid of Giza, turned it upside down and rammed it into the clay of the earth, the resulting hole would be something on the order of what you see when you stand behind the fence at Ground Zero. To the right, in one side of the canyon wall, an open tunnel leaks rusty water and slime onto the floor below. When the wind is calm there is still a stale odor in the air that must come from this place as it comes from a damp grave.

The walls of the pit are now reinforced concrete, and to the distance you may see level after level of orange barriers where work is started on a new building and memorial. Truly, this hole is a canyon in the middle of the city. At the bottom of the pit are the subway lines and the Cortland Street stop that used to connect with the WTC. Sometimes, when you take the subway farther downtown to the Staten Island Ferry, the motorman will slow the train here and announce over the intercom, "Formerly, the World Trade Center—Hallowed Ground."

The subway tunnels are draped now with metal sheeting, and seem like the arteries of a deep wound. Nearby, some of the buildings damaged by the explosions and fire on 9/11 are still being repaired. They, too, are draped in a protective tarp that looks from a distance like hanging, black gauze.

WILL IT BE FORGOTTEN?

Behind me I hear someone who pretends to be a guide explain what happened 3 years ago. He says, "The first plane slammed into the tower at nearly 500 miles an hour. The force of that impact made the building waver 17 feet." The man levels his palm as if it were an airplane and thrusts it into his other palm which is now perpendicular like a tower. The foreign tourists gathered around him nod in agreement. Who is he, I wonder? I guess he knows, but then at this ledge to darkness, who knows?

The U.S. is a big country. It holds both the silver of airports and the rust of railroad yards. You wonder if the wound that was 9/11 and the scar that is now Ground Zero resonates still in the hills of San Francisco or in the blue, desert sky above Phoenix. Do they remember it among the sea of dark green soy beans and corn on the Illinois prairie, or among the mist of the muddy Mississippi as the river winds around Algiers Point? You wonder as the sun goes down across the Hudson River if all this destruction is on its way to being redeemed or forgotten.

The war in Iraq and its aftermath is born from this pit dug into the lower end of Manhattan. For many Americans, those who have never been to New York City but fly the flag at the VFW post in a small Kansas town, the image of Sadam Hussein's statue hauled down from a square in Baghdad is small vengeance for the twin towers falling. Yet, for other Americans and some New Yorkers 9/11 is just an inconvenience to their lives of high fashion, caviar and dance. For them, politics scratches in the background like the white noise of a poorly tuned radio station.

That bright day in September 3 years ago was more than background noise for me. Like many who lived through the morning watching the news, that day was a stamp on our heart, an image we still see when we shut our eyes. Like a stone dropped into a pool, I suspect the ripples from that impact have not yet stopped their spread outward. But, in a few years a new tower 1,776 feet tall will stand here, one foot for every year up to the American Revolution. Then, as it always does, the New World will move on to something new. Perhaps by then someone who sees clearly from that height will come along and show us how that falling fits into the wide scheme of things.

On the ride back to the hotel, the subway car is full of young people going about their lives. I wonder if the towers falling will continue to be a vivid memory to those busy and trendy couples. Somehow, I feel 9/11 was more an event for the end of my generation, not the beginning of theirs. For many of my generation, this was a wound to our patriotism, something that left us all "violated."

The view of many young people who work or live here seems to be a different vision from mine. It seems to be a vision beyond America, something international and perhaps even forgiving. Yet, I look into their eyes and see like youth everywhere they carry with them the burden of the unknown. Do they hear in my voice an echo of midwestern sentimentalism? I wonder, too, if the politics of the young will protect them from the likes of this happening again. Even if all the animals dress like sheep, the wolf is still hungry.

STRANGE PARALLELS

The next morning I decide to go uptown to Times Square, Fort Tryon Park and The Cloisters. After Ground Zero, I am drawn first to this confusion of traffic and electricity, then go uptown and on to rugged greenery and a museum of medieval art. In two days I travel from one end of Manhattan to the other in search of ashes and light.

On a hot day in late July, Times Square still has the worn-out bustle of Bombay for me, except with more neon, video and ribbons of lettered signs that scroll as fast as I can read them. Americans from all over come here for this blatant display of materialism, arrogance and sometimes a desperate reaching after freedom and excellence. Can they fit anymore signs on the buildings, I ask myself and I walk to the subway at 42nd Street?

It is a noisy ride to 190th on the A train, but inside the stone rooms of The Cloisters there are places where it is dark, cool, and silent. This is always the condition of stone, until it is given life by carving. At the room dedicated to the southern French monastery of Saint-Guilhem Cloister, a series of stone capitols based on classical models surround the courtyard. What hope they had these men! How patient they were in transferring from life to stone all manner of persons and their deeds.

Looking at their fantastic art here, you feel that these anonymous men were always living on the eve of destruction. There is joy in the way a carved line makes a gentle "S," yet, there is severity in the lips, eyes and hands of their holy men. Do you suppose in their time they walked near the edge of their own Ground Zero? The guide book says, "Of particular interest in this arcade is that (capitol) representing the Last Judgment and the condemned souls descending into the mouth of hell."

The next day I set out for Chicago. It rains as the train leaves Penn Station and follows the Hudson River up to Albany. Raindrops scurry down the windowpane like frantic bugs. The sky is as gray as the polished gray rails that run parallel to my view. I remember sailing out of New York harbor years ago to the wide Atlantic. I watched then as the city's skyline disappeared on the evening horizon. Finally, miles at sea, there was nothing more but a dark stretch of land and two pillars jutting upward. They were the towers of the World Trade Center still visible. Now, I am going home. I have said my prayer. To the west, the entire country stretches out before me, from sea to shining sea.

The editors have compiled the following list of organizations concerned with the issues debated in this book. The descriptions are derived from materials provided by the organizations. All have publications or information available for interested readers. The list was compiled on the date of publication of the present volume; the information provided here may change. Be aware that many organizations take several weeks or longer to respond to inquiries, so allow as much time as possible.

AMERICAN CIVIL LIBERTIES UNION (ACLU)

125 Broad St., 18th Floor, New York, NY 10004-2400
(212) 549-2500
e-mail: aclu@aclu.org • Web site: www.aclu.org

The American Civil Liberties Union is a national organization that works to defend Americans' civil rights. The ACLU argues that measures to protect national security in the wake of terrorist attacks should not compromise civil liberties. Its publications include *Civil Liberties After 9-11: The ACLU Defends Freedom* and *National ID Cards: 5 Reasons Why They Should Be Rejected.*

ANTI-DEFAMATION LEAGUE (ADL)

823 United Nations Plaza, New York, NY 10017
(212) 885-7700 • fax: (212) 867-0779
Web site: www.adl.org

The Anti-Defamation League is a human relations organization that fights all forms of prejudice and bigotry. The Web site features extensive information on Israel, the Middle East, and terrorism, including information on terrorist groups and articles such as "Terrorism and Moral Clarity" and "Give Security Agencies More Room to Fight Terrorism." The ADL also publishes the bimonthly online newsletter *Frontline.*

BROOKINGS INSTITUTION

1775 Massachusetts Ave. NW, Washington, DC 20036
(202) 797-6000 • fax: (202) 797-6004
e-mail: brookinfo@brook.edu • Web site: www.brook.edu

The Brookings Institution conducts foreign policy research and analyzes global events and their impact on the United States. The institution publishes the *Brookings Review* quarterly, along with numerous papers and books on foreign policy. Publications related to terrorism include *Nasty, Brutish, and Long: America's War on Terrorism* and *Protecting the American Homeland: One Year On.*

CENTER FOR STRATEGIC AND INTERNATIONAL STUDIES (CSIS)

1800 K St. NW, Washington, DC 20006
(202) 887-0200 • fax: (202) 775-3199
Web site: www.csis.org

CSIS is a public policy research institution that focuses on America's economic policy, national security, and foreign and domestic policy. The center analyzes global crises and suggests U.S. military policies. Its publications include the journal *Washington Quarterly* and the studies *Protecting Against the Spread of Nuclear, Biological, and Chemical Weapons* and *Cyberthreats, Information Warfare, and Critical Infrastructure Protection: Defending the U.S. Homeland.*

COUNCIL ON AMERICAN-ISLAMIC RELATIONS (CAIR)

453 New Jersey Ave. SE, Washington, DC 20003
(202) 488-8787 • fax: (202) 488-0833
e-mail: cair@cair-net.org • Web site: www.cair-net.org

CAIR is a nonprofit organization that challenges stereotypes of Islam and Muslims and offers an Islamic perspective on public policy issues. Its publications include action alerts, news briefs, and the quarterly newsletter *Faith in Action.* The CAIR Web site features statements condemning both the September 11, 2001, terrorist attacks and subsequent discrimination against Muslims.

COUNCIL ON FOREIGN RELATIONS

58 E. Sixty-eighth St., New York, NY 10021
(212) 434-9400 • fax: (212) 434-9800
e-mail: communications@cfr.org • Web site: www.cfr.org

The council researches the international aspects of American economic and political policies. Its journal *Foreign Affairs*, published five times a year, provides analysis on global conflicts. Publications relating to terrorism include the anthology *The War on Terror*, the report *Threats to Democracy: Prevention and Response*, and various articles.

GLOBAL EXCHANGE

2017 Mission St., #303, San Francisco, CA 94110
(415) 255-7296 • fax: (415) 255-7498
Web site: www.globalexchange.org

Global Exchange is a human rights organization that aims to expose economic and political injustice. It believes the best solution to such injustices is education, activism, and a noninterventionist U.S. foreign policy. Global Exchange opposes military retaliation in response to terrorist attacks. Books on terrorism are available for purchase on its Web site, and the organization also publishes a quarterly newsletter.

INTERNATIONAL POLICY INSTITUTE FOR COUNTER-TERRORISM (ICT)

PO Box 167, Herzlia, 46150, Israel
972-9-9527277 • fax: 972-9-9513073
e-mail: info@ict.org.il • Web site: www.ict.org.il

ICT is a research institute that develops public policy solutions to international terrorism. Its Web site is a comprehensive resource on terrorism and counter-terrorism, including an extensive database on terrorist organizations. Numerous articles on terrorism are published on the site, including "The Continuing Al-Qaida Threat" and "The Changing Threat of International Terrorism."

MIDDLE EAST RESEARCH AND INFORMATION PROJECT (MERIP)

1500 Massachusetts Ave. NW, Suite 119, Washington, DC 20005
(202) 223-3677 • fax: (202) 223-3604
e-mail: ctoensing@merip.org • Web site: www.merip.org

MERIP is a nonprofit organization that has no ties to any religious, political, or educational organization. The project believes that stereotypes and misconceptions have kept the United States and Europe from fully understanding the Middle East. MERIP aims to end this misunderstanding by addressing a wide range of political, cultural, and social issues and by publishing writings by authors from the Middle East. MERIP publishes the quarterly magazine *Middle East Report*, op-ed pieces, and *Middle East Report Online*, which includes Web-only analysis and commentary.

NATIONAL MEMORIAL INSTITUTE FOR THE PREVENTION OF TERRORISM (MIPT)

PO Box 889, Oklahoma City, OK 73101
(405) 232-5121 • fax: (405) 232-5132
Web site: www.mipt.org

According to its mission statement, MIPT is "dedicated to preventing terrorism or mitigating its effects." It was organized from a desire of survivors and families of victims of the Oklahoma City bombing to establish a living memorial and to ensure that other cities would not have to suffer through terrorist acts. To this end, MIPT researches the political and social causes of terrorism and makes the information available to interested parties. It has also amassed one of the largest libraries on terrorism-related research materials. In addition, the institute publishes several books and fact sheets on terrorism, parts of which are available for viewing online.

TERRORISM RESEARCH CENTER

(877) 635-0816
e-mail: TRC@terrorism.com • Web site: www.terrorism.com

The goal of the Terrorism Research Center is to inform the public on terrorism and information warfare. The site features profiles of terrorist organizations, essays and analysis, and links to other terrorism-related documents and resources.

U.S. DEPARTMENT OF STATE COUNTERTERRORISM OFFICE

Office of the Coordinator for Counterterrorism
Office of Public Affairs, Room 2509, U.S. Department of State
2201 C St. NW, Washington, DC 20520
(202) 647-4000
e-mail: http://contact-us.state.gov

The U.S. Department of State is a federal agency that advises the president on foreign policy matters. The Office of Counterterrorism publishes the annual report *Patterns of Global Terrorism*, a list of the United States' most wanted terrorists, and numerous fact sheets and press releases on the war on terrorism.

WASHINGTON INSTITUTE FOR NEAR EAST POLICY

1828 L St. NW, Suite 1050, Washington, DC 20036
(202) 452-0650 • fax: (202) 223-5364
e-mail: info@washingtoninstitute.org • Web site: www.washingtoninstitute.org

The institute is an independent organization that researches and analyzes Middle Eastern issues and U.S. policy in the region. Its Web site features several publications on terrorism, including the anthology *America and the Middle East—Expanding Threat, Broadening Response* and several PolicyWatches, among them "Patterns of Terrorism 2002."

BOOKS

Mellina Fanouris, *Phaedra*. Nairobi, Kenya: Kul Graphics, 2003.

Mitchell Fink and Lois Mathias, eds., *Never Forget: An Oral History of September 11, 2001*. New York: Regan, 2002.

Bruce Hoffman, *Inside Terrorism*. New York: Columbia University Press, 1998.

David Hoffman, *The Oklahoma City Bombing and the Politics of Terror*. Venice, CA: Feral House, 1998.

Rex Hudson, *Who Becomes a Terrorist and Why: The 1999 Government Report on Profiling Terrorists*. Guilford, CT: Lyons, 2002.

Pinhas Inbari, *The Palestinians: Between Terrorism and Statehood*. Brighton, UK: Sussex Academic Press, 1996.

Mark Kukis, *My Heart Became Attached: The Strange Journey of John Walker Lindh*. Washington, DC: Brassey's, 2003.

Robert Jay Lifton, *Destroying the World to Save It: Aum Shinrikyo, Apocalyptic Violence, and the New Global Terrorism*. New York: Metropolitan, 1999.

Lou Michel and Dan Herbeck, *American Terrorist: Timothy McVeigh and the Tragedy at Oklahoma City*. New York: Regan, 2001.

Haruki Murakami, *Underground: The Tokyo Gas Attack and the Japanese Psyche*. Trans. Alfred Birnbaum and Philip Gabriel. London: Harvill, 2000.

Dean E. Murphy, ed., *September 11: An Oral History*. New York: Doubleday, 2002.

National Commission on Terrorist Attacks, *The 9/11 Commission Report: Final Report of the National Commission on Terrorist Attacks upon the United States*. New York: W.W. Norton, 2004.

Paul R. Pillar, *Terrorism and U.S. Foreign Policy*. Washington, DC: Brookings Institution, 2003.

Gail Sheehy, *Middletown, America: One Town's Passage from Trauma to Hope.* New York: Random House, 2003.

Jessica Stern, *Terror in the Name of God: Why Religious Militants Kill.* New York: Ecco, 2003.

PERIODICALS

Catherine Arnst, "How the War on Terror Is Damaging the Brain Pool," *Business Week*, May 19, 2003.

Peter Bergen, "The Long Hunt for Osama," *Atlantic Monthly*, October 2004.

Christopher DeMuth, "Guns, Butter, and the War on Terror," *Wall Street Journal*, April 29, 2004.

David W. Dunlap, "A Reflective View at Ground Zero, with Images from Your Sponsors," *New York Times*, August 19, 2004.

Economist, "The Enemy Within," October 9, 2004.

———, "Plots, Alarms, and Arrests—Chasing al-Qaeda," August 14, 2004.

John Geedes, "Are We Safe Enough?" *Maclean's*, October 25, 2004.

Alberto R. Gonzales, "Terrorists Are Different," *USA Today*, June 10, 2004.

Michael Isikoff, Michael Hirsh, Mark Hosenball, and Steve Tuttle, "9/11: The Iran Factor," *Newsweek*, July 26, 2004.

James Kelly, "What Happened That Day on Patrol," *Time*, December 29, 2003.

Jenna M. McKnight, "In a Speck of 9/11 Dust, a World of Chaos," *New York Times*, September 7, 2004.

Ami Pedazhur, Arie Perliger, and Leonard Weinberg, "Altruism and Fatalism: The Characteristics of Palestinian Suicide Terrorists," *Deviant Behavior*, July 2003.

Robert Reeg, "The Twin Towers Fall," *American History*, October 2004.

Amin Saikal, "Struggle for the Global Soul," *World Today*, August/September 2004.

Murray Sayle, "Nerve Gas and the Four Noble Truths," *New Yorker*, April 1, 1996.

William F. Schulz, "Security Is a Human Right, Too?" *New York Times Magazine*, April 18, 2004.

P.W. Singer, "The War on Terrorism," *Current*, September 2004.

Marc Steyn, "The Future of Jihad," *National Review*, September 13, 2004.

USA Today, "Iraq, War on Terror Cast Shadow Around the Globe," September 30, 2004.

George Wehfritz, Hideko Takayama, and Kay Itoi, "From Sarin to Software," *Newsweek*, March 13, 2000.

Patricia J. Williams, "Unimagined Communities," *Nation*, May 3, 2004.

Lee Kuan Yew, "Terrorism Escalates Worldwide," *Forbes*, October 18, 2004.